Voices of a Nomadic Soul

Zbigniew Kotowicz

FERNANDO PESSOA:

VOICES OF A NOMADIC SOUL

Shearsman Books & The Menard Press
Exeter   London

This revised edition is published in the United Kingdom in 2008 by

Shearsman Books Ltd   and   The Menard Press
58 Velwell Road   8 The Oaks
Exeter EX4 4LD   Woodside Avenue
                                                    London N12 8AR

First published in 1996 by
The Menard Press and King's College London.

www.shearsman.com

ISBN 978-1-905700-31-8

Acknowledgements
'Maritime Ode', 'Opium Eater', 'Salutation to Walt Whitman', 'Lisbon
Revisited (1923)', 'Lisbon Revisited (1926)', 'I love and animate every-
thing...' from *Poems of Fernando Pessoa* translated and edited by Edwin Honig
and Susan M. Brown. First published by Ecco Press in 1986. Reprinted by
permission.

Ten extracts from *The Keeper of Flocks* by Fernando Pessoa, from *The
Complete Poems of Alberto Caeiro*, Shearsman Books, Exeter. Copyright ©
2007 by Chris Daniels. Reprinted by permission of the translator.

The author would like to thank the following for kindly giving
permission to use their translations in this work: Jean Longland, Suzette
Macedo, Peter Rickard, Richard Zenith. Acknowledgments too to the
Edinburgh University Press for translations of Peter Rickard, and to
Anthony Rudolf, literary executor of Jonathan Griffin, for the latter's
translations.

Contents

PREFACE TO THE SECOND EDITION

This text was written a little over ten years ago. Since then, new translations of Pessoa's writings have appeared, and scholarship has evolved. Consequently, in this new edition most of the translations of poems and of *The Book of Disquiet* have been replaced. Apart from corrections of misprints, odd punctuation and syntactical wobbles and a few re-written sentences, the text remains unchanged, except for the last section in which I update the account of editorial activities around Pessoa's work.

The first edition owed its appearance to José Blanco, at the time at Calouste Gulbenkian Foundation in Lisbon, through whom I was given a generous grant to research for this book, and to Anthony Rudolf of the Menard Press who saw fit to publish it (again with assistance from the Gulbenkian Foundation). When I was working on it, I was fortunate enough to meet and discuss Pessoa with some who already had intimate knowledge of his work. José Blanco, who is perhaps the leading authority on bibliographical matters, read this text in the earlier stages; many conversations with the now-retired Professor Luís de Sousa Rebelo of King's College, London were of great help to me; Richard Zenith, an editor and translator of Pessoa's writings was another interlocutor. Kate Chalkley and Aldous Eveleigh were my 'non-professional' readers. I thank them again for their help.

Lisbon,
September 2007

I

Everything stated or expressed by man is a note in the
margin of a completely erased text. From what's in the
note we can extract the gist of what must have been
in the text, but there's always a doubt, and the possible
meanings are many.

The Book of Disquiet

An encounter with Pessoa is unsettling. About the only thing
that almost never changed were the insignia: a hat, a bow tie,
spectacles and the moustache. The rest was elusive, slipping
away like a snake. A solitary insomniac, at odds with himself
and others, a chain-smoker, heavy drinker, unsmiling and
meticulously dressed, he bombards us with contradictions and
paradoxes. He created fictional poets, wrote political pamphlets,
penned one of this century's great confessionals. Each time we
look at him we see something different. Today Fernando Pessoa
is recognized as one of the great figures of Modernism but he
still remains an enigma.

Pessoa was born in Lisbon in 1888. When he was five he lost
his father. Two years later his mother married the Portuguese
vice-consul in Durban, South Africa, and the young Pessoa
moved to live there. He returned alone to Lisbon when he was
seventeen and the following years were a mixture of restlessness
and immobility. For over a decade he changed address more than
once a year; then, when his mother, a widow again, returned
to Lisbon, he moved in with her and the rest of the family and
he never budged again. He ventured out of Lisbon only twice,
on trips to provincial towns. He had some friends, though not
many, most of them also poets. He never married and the sole
amorous liaison that Pessoa is known to have had lasted all of
a few months, was rekindled for another brief spell almost ten
years later, and left for posterity some poignant love letters.

After returning from South Africa to Lisbon, Pessoa enrolled at the university. This he gave up almost at once to venture, with a little inheritance, into publishing. The money was quickly lost and Pessoa finally settled as translator of foreign correspondence for business firms. At one point he considered setting himself up as an astrologer and two years before he died he applied for the job of a librarian, which he did not get. Translating business letters (and a few books) was Pessoa's only professional activity.

All his life Pessoa was in emotional and spiritual turmoil. He often feared going insane and at certain periods contemplated putting himself in a lunatic asylum. This turmoil may have had something to do with the number of deaths that he experienced when still very young—his father, a brother, a half-brother, and a half-sister. And death followed him later. His closest friend, the poet Mario de Sá-Carneiro committed suicide, Spanish flu took away some leading artists with whom Pessoa worked together. He also knew insanity from close up. When in his late teens, Pessoa lived for some months with a grandmother who was apparently completely unhinged.

A psychoanalyst would find plenty to speculate on but otherwise there is not much to excite a biographer. Pessoa would reply, like many have before him and many since, that his life is in his work, nowhere else. Writing meant to Pessoa everything. He wrote on any subject that came his way, he wrote when sober and when drunk, in notebooks and on all sorts of scraps of paper. When he could not write he suffered and he also suffered when he wrote. Pessoa left behind a trunk stuffed with manuscripts and when researchers laid their hands on it, they discovered that it contained poetry, prose, literary criticism, philosophical remarks, mysticism, astrology, aesthetics, morals, psychology, lists of projected books, writings for a commerce periodical, a guide to Lisbon and much more. According to the official count there are in all 27,543 documents that make up the Pessoa archive.

A huge Pessoa industry has since developed. Literary critics, psychologists, philosophers and others have been deciphering a miscellany of personal notes, rough drafts, letters, abandoned projects, as well as completed but unpublished works. For decades after his death new poems and prose pieces have been coming out in print. This posthumous activity could lead one to think that, like Kafka, or Bruno Schulz, Pessoa was known in his life to no more than a handful of friends and fellow writers. Not quite true. When he died, in 1935, his reputation was considerable: translations into French had already appeared, and one of the leading national newspapers *Diário de Notícias* announced his death on its front page with a photograph and the title 'Death of a Great Portuguese Poet'. Pessoa was reticent and timid in his personal life but his literary life was active and he was not at all shy when it came to creating his public persona. He published regularly and he was careful about what he published. His literary biography is very intriguing. Here are some of the significant signposts:

Pessoa makes his first appearance in 1912 with three polemical articles on the state of Portuguese literature. The next three years he continues with polemical interventions and in 1914 he publishes his first few poems. 1915 is a watershed year. With a group of avant-garde poets and painters Pessoa runs two issues of an influential modernist review *Orpheu*. He publishes in *Orpheu* six poems entitled 'Oblique Rain', a 'static drama' *The Mariner* and, under the name of a certain Álvaro de Campos, three long poems: 'Opium Eater', 'Maritime Ode', 'Triumphal Ode'. In the same year Pessoa writes more polemical articles and he undertakes the translation of several volumes of theosophical works of Besant, Leadbeater and Blavatsky. In 1916 a series of poems *Stations of the Cross* appears and more translations of theosophical works. In 1917, with some people from the *Orpheu* group, Pessoa is involved in another avant-garde review (seized by the police as soon as it appeared) *Portugal Futurista*. Here Pessoa publishes some poems and a provocative manifesto 'Ultimatum' signed by

Álvaro de Campos. In 1918 he brings out a slim volume of English poems, in 1920 a long poem 'In Memory of President-King Sidónio Pais', in 1922 a cycle of poems *Portuguese Sea*, a piece in prose *The Anarchist Banker* and two more volumes of English poetry—all of these under his own name. In 1923 a new poem by Álvaro de Campos appears and three poems in French. In 1924 a new name enters: Ricardo Reis, with twenty of his Odes. The next year Pessoa introduces still another name: Alberto Caeiro, with a selection from a cycle *The Keeper of Flocks* and other poems. Between 1925 and 1934 sporadic poems signed by Pessoa, Reis, Campos and Caeiro find their way into various periodicals; further polemical interventions appear, some of them on matters of literature, some political, the most notorious an article from 1928: 'The Interregnum. Defence and Justification of Military Dictatorship in Portugal'. In 1934 Pessoa publishes his only book of Portuguese poems *Message* for which he is awarded a national prize. The following year he writes in a daily newspaper an article in defence of Masonry which was coming under increasing attack from the government. The same year Pessoa dies of a sudden attack of hepatitis, which means that he more or less drank himself to death. He was forty-seven.

This is a very eccentric list. Political and artistic interventions and a most unusual poetic output—poems in English and in French as well as in Portuguese, many of them written under different names. Each time we seem to be reading a distinctly different poet. Alberto Cairo's *The Keeper of Flocks* is a cycle of quiet bucolic poems, Ricardo Reis is a classicist who imitates Horace and Álvaro de Campos is a manic, free verse, sometimes Whitmanesque poet. When Pessoa wrote under his own name he differed just as much. 'Oblique Rain' reads like a poetic attempt at cubism, with intersecting and parallel sensations brought into a single poetic stream; *Stations of the Cross* is a series of occult poems; 'In Memory of the President-King Sidónio Pais' and *Message*, which includes most of the poems from the earlier *Portuguese Sea*, are intensely patriotic. We are confronted with disjointed voices belonging to different discourses, written in different languages coming under different names.

Pessoa cultivated this multiplicity and he explained it in different ways. According to one account this was a sign of a psychological anomaly, which went way back to childhood. Already when he was six he would write letters to himself under the guise of someone else. From then on he lived with a multitude of voices, discourses, personalities and this at times drove him mad. These imaginary people, usually writers, were given names and they wrote on different subjects and in different languages. There was an António Mora who speculated on metaphysics, there was an Alexander Search who wrote only in English, and there were many others, including the poets Alberto Caeiro, Álvaro de Campos and Ricardo Reis. According to another explanation Pessoa experienced metempsychotic phenomena. He felt within himself, like a medium, the presence of others; 'it happens, that when looking in the mirror, I see my face disappear and a face of a bearded man emerge, or of another one (there are four in all that appear this way)', he confided in a letter. His lifelong fascination with the occult, Theosophy, and Rosicrucianism seems connected with these. He wrote occult poems, he experimented with automatic writing and the occult theme comes up in many unexpected places in Pessoa's work.

Whatever the origins of this multiplicity Pessoa also worked out and published an aesthetical doctrine of a multiple personality. This came from Álvaro de Campos. In 1917, in the review *Portugal Futurista*, Campos published a lively manifesto 'Ultimatum'. Influenced by the rhetoric of Futurism, Campos launched into a tirade about the decadent state of European culture, 'I, of the Race of Navigators, . . . I, of the Race of Discoverers, . . . I am going to show you the Way.' He knows what the future holds: 'Science teaches . . . that each of us is an assembly of subsidiary psyches, a badly-made synthesis of cellular souls. For the Christian self-feeling, the most perfect man is the man who is most coherent with himself; for the man

15

of science, the most perfect is the man who is most incoherent with himself'. An artist should work towards an 'abolition of the dogma of artistic individuality. The greater the artist, the less definable he is, and he will write in more genres with more contradictions and dissimilarities'. In an undated fragment which later found its way into *The Book of Disquiet* Pessoa wrote: 'I'd like to write the encomium of a new incoherence that could serve as the negative charter for the new anarchy of souls.'

Pessoa acted out these postulates. Alberto Caeiro, Ricardo Reis and Álvaro de Campos are the result. He was probably the first to subject the notion of 'I' to such radical scrutiny. How many am I? Am I the subject or object of speech? Is there a real author? We are multiple, incoherent and contradictory. A unified identity, a definable personality or subjectivity is an illusion. Today this would be recognized as a post-modernist programme and one could thus claim that Pessoa anticipated certain philosophical debates by more than half a century. This is to an extent true only that the matter is not so simple. Some of the contradictions in Pessoa are troubling. One would like to understand how it is that the same person writes some beautiful modern poems, like the Odes of Álvaro de Campos, and also writes and publishes the unattractive 'In memory of President-King Sidónio Pais', an esoteric poem which mourns the death of a president who rather than being a king was a dictator. Then again, the same Campos publishes 'Ultimatum'—a manifesto for new art and a few years later Pessoa, under his own name, writes 'The Interregnum. The Justification and Defence of Military Dictatorship'—the title is self-explanatory. Campos and Pessoa were speaking to completely different audiences, audiences which ascribe to conflicting values. Of this Pessoa was well aware as is obvious from his publishing practices. Campos began his activities in the scandalous, modernist review *Orpheu*, the poem to Sidónio Pais and 'The Interregnum' appeared in a right-wing monarchist periodical *Acçao, Órgão do Núcleo de Acção Nacional*. It somehow does not seem satisfactory to explain this away with a claim that one is multiple and that therefore, at one time or another, or simultaneously, one holds different, inconsistent views. Nor is it satisfactory to put it down as a sign of neurasthenia or metempsychotic experiences.

The particular set where modernist and reactionary forces co-exist is a raw nerve that shows in Pessoa's generation throughout Europe. The period is referred to loosely as Modernism. From Lisbon to Moscow artists were announcing a rebellion against old values. New horizons were opening. Literature, fine arts, music, as well as science, were undergoing profound changes. The number of avant-garde movements and artists involved in them is staggering and this century's greatest hopes were associated with these developments. Pessoa knew only a little about them but he firmly belonged there. And at the same time, from Lisbon to Moscow, political forces were brewing that turned this century into a horror. As it turned out, there were artists who were touched by both, who showed an enthusiasm for ideologies which were in blatant contradiction to the spirit in which they created their art. Amongst the most illustrious we find fascists, warmongers, misogynists, anti-semites, eulogists of Stalinism. Suicides, premature deaths, lunatic asylums are frequent entries in the biographies of artists of that period.

It so happens that in order to make sense of Pessoa the poet it is also necessary to have some understanding of his political and ideological beliefs. The matter is of particular interest because it has to do with a writer's relation to History. The way in which Pessoa was entangled with his country's spiritual, political and artistic past shaped his poetic destiny and it explains a great deal about the contradictions that are so much part of his project. It may also be that in unravelling his story we will be saying something about the others.

Pessoa entered the world of literature with a series of three polemical articles—of a political, sociological and historical bent—on the state of Portuguese poetry. In the first, entitled

'New Portuguese Poetry Sociologically Considered', Pessoa predicts a coming of a very fertile period. A poet, or several poets, of such quality will appear that they will push Portugal's great bard Luís de Camões into the background. He says:

> One can argue that the current political movement is not of a type to generate supreme poetic geniuses, as it is vulgar and mean. But *it is precisely for that reason* that we arrive more easily at the conclusion that a Supra-Camões will arrive in our land.

Pessoa did not claim that he would be the Supra-Camões but it is quite certain that he saw himself in this role. Shortly afterwards he wrote in an autobiographical note: 'I have come to a full possession of my Genius and have a divine consciousness of my Mission'. To say that this is akin to announcing in England the imminent arrival of a supra-Shakespeare, or in Italy of a supra-Dante would still be an understatement. Camões's place in Portuguese history is doubly important. He was a great poet and he belonged to and is a symbol of his country's golden age—the Great Discoveries of the fifteenth and sixteenth centuries. His epic *The Lusiads* is a paean to that age.

Almost a century earlier than anyone else the Portuguese were launching sea expeditions. Within a few decades they explored the West Coast of Africa, found the sea route to India, discovered Brazil, established a foothold in China, reached Japan, Sumatra, Java, Timor. They were the first to circumnavigate the earth. Vasco da Gama, Pedro Álvares Cabral, Fernão de Magalhães (Magellan), to mention only a few, gave navigation an altogether new dimension. They laid the world open, and the Portuguese reaped rich profits from it. But there was more to it than just the glory of Portugal. This small nation was showing the rest of Europe how to go about colonising faraway lands. In Prince Henry the Navigator, who for forty years organized the first sea expeditions, they had the prototype of a Minister of Overseas Affairs; they had the geographical knowledge; they had the navigators, soldiers to secure the routes militarily, merchants to organize the trade; they had the first colonialist administrators. Greeks gave us culture, Romans the law, the Portuguese taught Europe how to expand.

Camões's life is very much part of that tale. He spends his youth as a soldier, troublemaker, womaniser and court poet. He takes part in some Crusade expedition in North Africa and loses an eye. Back in Lisbon after a brawl he ends up for a short while in prison. Later, to escape it all, he joins the King's service as a soldier and is shipped off to India to join the colonialist administration. He is away for sixteen years. During this time he is shipwrecked in China, imprisoned in Goa, stranded in Mozambique and throughout he hangs on to the one possession that mattered to him most—the manuscript of *The Lusiads*. Three years after his return, the epic is published and recognition is almost immediate, but not by the then reigning King Sebastian who Camões dedicated the work to. So court recognition (and financial rewards with it) did not come and all that Camões was given was a pension for his services to the king in the colonies. The pension was meagre, paid irregularly and Camões died poor.

Camões set out to give Portugal a poetic voice to match its political greatness. He was well versed in classics, which suggests that he studied in Coimbra. He knew Virgil as well as the Florentines, Dante and Petrarch. He set out to create a Portuguese epic that would rival them. The title *The Lusiads* carries analogies with *The Iliad* and *The Aeneid*, it fixes a lineage to the legendary Lusus from whom the Portuguese believed themselves to be descended, and it is in the plural—this is not a story about one heroic individual but about a people. And, unlike *The Iliad* and *The Aeneid*, which deal with the mythical past, Camões took as his raw material the most recent history, the Great Discoveries. The theme of the poem is Vasco da Gama's first voyage to India. The epic follows da Gama's route along the African coast, around the Cape of Good Hope and across the Indian Ocean to their destination. Travelling through territory controlled by the Muslims—some devious, some trustworthy—they find friendly pilots, they get to India and they escape at the last moment. The other adversary, perhaps the most formidable, is the sea. It comes in the shape of the giant sea monster Adamastor, the most enduring image of *The Lusiads*. Adamastor bars the sailors' way around the Cape of Good Hope and is defeated by their will. The Portuguese navigate around the cape and lay the ocean open; they are the first masters of the sea.

The Lusiads is complex and ambiguous. Although it comes from a later period it belongs to the Renaissance when the new Christian God still had to co-exist with the older Greek pantheon. Camões mixed the two without any embarrassment. So, the sailors extol their God, it is in His name that they travel and conquer, and they pray to Him. The prayers are answered by Venus who favours the children of Lusus, and it is she who steers them through all the dangers. Camões is a Christian and a good patriot but he does not send Vasco da Gama home to stately honours, instead, through the good services of Venus, the sailors end their adventure on an Island of Love where each one of them finds his nymph. The heroes are rewarded with an orgy fit for the gods. Already at the second edition the Inquisition's scissors were busy at work.

Camões sang a hymn to his country's achievements when in fact Portugal's grandeur was coming to a rapid end. He already sensed the malaise that was setting in, there are passages in *The Lusiads* that attest to this, but he would have never predicted the swiftness of the decline. In 1580, only a few years after the epic was published and just weeks before Camões died, Portugal lost its independence to Spain and the mighty colonialist power crashed. The dream was over. Camões's poetry was the last great deed of the epoch. He gave the nation of navigators, soldiers and colonialists a poetic voice of European stature.

Pessoa's attitude to Camões was complex. In a letter he wrote:

> I have great admiration for Camões (the epic, not the lyric) but I do not know of any Camonian element that would have had an influence on me, though I am easily influenced. [. . .] What Camões could have taught me I had already learned from others.

This is probably the only time when Pessoa 'admires' Camões. All other remarks, and there are not many, tend to be disparaging and belittling. In one comment Pessoa thinks that Camões was not able to appreciate the greatness of his age because he did not have the necessary distance from it. One can only appreciate the immensity of the Himalaya from far away, or in the memory, or from the imagination, wrote Pessoa at one point, and added: 'There is only one period of creation in our literary history: it has not arrived yet'. Shakespeare, Virgil, Milton, Dickens, Baudelaire, Wordsworth, Dante, Goethe, Shelly, Blake, Byron, Coleridge, Hugo—this cosmopolitan assembly is the list of people that Pessoa singles out for respect. No place for Camões there. As far as Pessoa is concerned Camões is not really particularly important even in Portuguese literature; there are many poets he rates more highly. If Pessoa admired Camões it was a grudging admiration. But grudging or not, Pessoa seemed serious in his intention to produce poetry that would surpass Camões. And since he predicted the arrival of several poets that would remove the Bard from the pedestal he also seemed to quite literally take upon himself the creation of the several poets whose task it would be. Álvaro de Campos, Alberto Caeiro and Ricardo Reis, the three fictional poets created by Pessoa, were at least in one sense conceived that way. Pessoa hoped that the activities of the group of young poets who edited with him *Orpheu* and later *Portugal Futurista* would elevate Portuguese poetry into European prominence. He was writing endless presentations, often in English, to introduce the movement in Europe. Some time after *Portugal Futurista*, Pessoa thought of setting up a literary review, a sort of Portuguese Poetic Offensive, which

would be published alternately in French and in English. He
intended to use all three, Caeiro, Campos and Reis, because,
as he explained in a letter, 'this break-up into pseudonymic
personalities is moreover more necessary as, for the moment,
there is (almost) no-one *numerically*.' Why would numbers be
needed? Perhaps Pessoa recognized that no one single poet
could hope to match Camões. Camões wrote in an age where
the world was still felt as one, where God, the Greek pantheon,
love, patriotism could dwell together. That was before religious
wars tore the continent apart. Today no such thing is possible.
It would take several to encompass a world such as Camões's.
And it is interesting to note that Caeiro, Campos and Reis, put
together, have something of Camões's spread. Campos throws
himself into everything with an insatiable thirst for sensation,
Reis is a quiet classicist who welcomes the pagan gods, Caeiro
loves nature. They and Pessoa himself would do what Camões
had done; they would give Portuguese poetry prominence.

Álvaro de Campos was entrusted to lead the mission. He
belongs to the Race of Navigators and Discoverers, he proudly
declared in 'Ultimatum'. In 1915, the year which was so prolific,
more poetry came from Campos than from Pessoa under his
own name. He was unleashed onto the public with 'Triumphal
Ode'—a Whitmanesque, free-verse, futurist, machine-loving
howl—described once as the loudest poem ever written.
Then came the quieter 'Opium Eater' and Whitman again in
'Maritime Ode'. The last of these occupies a special place in
Pessoa's work. It is the longest poem that he ever wrote, one
of the finest, and special because it is here that we find a direct
engagement with Camões.

'Maritime Ode' is an imaginary sea voyage. Standing on
the dock Campos watches the steamers coming in and out of
the harbour. He falls into a reverie.

And I am swaddled, as with the memory of some other person
Mysteriously become my own.

Well, who knows, who knows,
If once, way back, before me,
I did not leave from such a dock; if I, a ship
In the sun's slanting dawn light,
Did not depart from some other port?

The first two lines are of a kind that appear in many of Pessoa's poems. He experiences in himself someone else; the metempsychotic powers are at work. In the other poems the lives that invade Pessoa are mysterious; they are of the occult world. In this instance one is inclined to think that this other person is not so mysterious, that in fact it could be Camões himself as the poem re-lives the adventures of the early navigators.

To wake up to days more immediate than any in Europe,
To see mysterious ports on the wide wastes of ocean,
To round distant capes and come upon sudden vast
    landscapes
Past countless stunning hillsides . . .

I would love to see again before me only schooners and ships
    built of timber,
And hear of no other maritime life than the old seafaring life!

'Maritime Ode' enters the territory of *The Lusiads*: the sea. But this is not an imitation: if anything, it is a challenge to Camões. *The Lusiads* may be an epic that describes a real adventure, it may be the greatest achievement in Portuguese literature, but it is also a mystification. Camões beautified and sanitised da Gama's voyage. Vasco da Gama was not rewarded with an island of love. The actual thing was hard, full of toil and violence—less than half the crew got back home; among the dead was da Gama's brother Paulo. Those who did return were in no fit condition to celebrate. 'Maritime Ode' is a dream of the savagery of the early voyages:

You men who raised stone pillars to mark the coasts, you
     who named the capes!
Who first traded with Negroes!
Who first sold slaves from new lands!
Who gave the astonished Negresses their first European
     orgasm!
You who brought back gold, glass beads, fragrant woods,
  arrows,
From hillsides exploding with green vegetation!
You men who plundered peaceful African villages,
Scattering the natives with the roar of your cannon,
You who murdered, robbed, tortured, and grabbed the booty
Of the New, thanks to those who with lowered heads
Crushed the mystery of the newfound seas! Hey, hey, hey!
To all of you together, to all of you as though you were one,
To all of you mixed together and interlocking,
To all of you bloody, violent, hated, feared, revered,
I salute you, I salute you, I salute you!

Camões lost an eye in war. For 16 years he lived the hard life
of those first explorers; his travels and his return home were of
almost Odyssean proportions—there is enough there to write
another epic—but *The Lusiads* is unreal. Pessoa reverses values.
He does not travel, he is timid and immobile, but his imaginary
sensation is real. The superiority of imaginary over real travel
was a poetic imperative to which Pessoa held on consistently
all his life. In 'Opium Eater', another poem of Campos from
the same early period, this imperative is articulated clearly and
the reference to Camões seems unmistakable:

I think it's not worth having gone
To the Orient, seen India and China.
The earth is always so small and the same.
And there is only one way to live.

'Maritime Ode' announces a radical departure from Camões.
It breaks the myth of *The Lusiads*; it breaks with the past. And,
just to make sure that this departure is complete, Pessoa rejects

the poetic idiom of his day. So while Camões, faithful to the spirit of his age, followed the masters and adopted for his epic the intricate and precise *ottava rima* of Ariosto, Campos takes as his mentor Walt Whitman, the first who was to sing in free verse. Campos was really a scandal.

Campos opened the mission to unseat Camões; Alberto Caeiro and Ricardo Reis would follow. They really meant a great deal to Pessoa. He wrote to a poet friend: 'Everything that I have written under the names of Caeiro, Reis and Álvaro de Campos is serious. Through all three of them I let a deep conception pass, different in each but in each the concern about the mysterious importance of the simple fact of existing'. This was in 1915; the poems were ready and it seems that, after Campos, Pessoa was getting ready to launch the other two. But this is not what happened. Instead Pessoa became immersed in a powerful Portuguese myth, a myth that was born around the same time that Camões wrote *The Lusiads*.

Camões dedicated *The Lusiads* to King Sebastian. Who was he? The historical accounts describe him as a gloomy man, a religious zealot; he was probably mentally unstable. His reign ended in Portugal's greatest ever disaster.

Sebastian ascended the throne in 1557 while still a young boy. Educated by the Jesuits he grew up obsessed with the idea of a crusade. His fanaticism was to prove just as strong as that of his uncle, the vindictive Philip II of Spain. While the Spanish were battling with heretical Holland, Sebastian had his eyes turned to the Arabs. Finally, in 1578, he undertook an ill-advised military campaign in Morocco. The battle in the sands of Alcazar Kebir was a calamity—Sebastian went down with the best of Portuguese nobility. He left no heir. Two years later Philip II, one of the claimants to the throne, entered Lisbon and Portugal fell into Spanish hands. Almost overnight, Portugal, the greatest colonialist power, with jurisdiction over half the world, became a subjugated nation. The country had to wait sixty years before it regained independence. As in a Greek tragedy, the rise and fall were the destiny of one royal family, the House of Avis. It began with João I, the father of Henry the Navigator, and ended with the folly of Sebastian.

King Sebastian lost the battle of Alcazar Kebir but his body was never found and no one saw him slain. This gave birth to Portugal's most powerful and enduring myth: one day Sebastian, The Hidden One, *O Encoberto*, would return emerging from a morning mist and restore Portugal's greatness. Independence came but not the former glory, and the yearning for Sebastian remained. It evolved into a belief in his return in a new incarnation, a messiah who would come and lead the Portuguese again.

The myth is complex and it was quite long in the making. It began even before Sebastian's Moroccan adventure. Portugal was already crumbling. The country had been falling increasingly under the influence of Madrid, which was the centre of religious zeal. The Spanish had an insatiable crusading drive; they fought for the purity of faith on all fronts. They were sending missionaries to the newly discovered faraway lands, they continued to fight the Arabs, they were engaged in battle with Protestant Holland, and they "purified" their own land by expelling the Jews. Portugal began acting in similar fashion. Two years after the Spanish they also ordered the Jews out. The results were pretty much the same—persecution, massacre and a loss of a great number of wealthy and educated citizens. Corruption at home, exploitation abroad, the unrest after the expulsion of the Jews—there were many signs of decadence. In fact, all of Europe was being shaken by religious ferment. This was the age of Nostradamus and Portugal also had its prophets. The best known was a cobbler, Gonçalo Anes Bandarra. His songs and ditties spoke of a coming new era when the faith would be pure and strife overcome. He became very popular and attracted enquiries from the Inquisition. He was arrested and then released as a harmless fool; "good for keeping sheep" was the Holy Office's verdict. After the loss of independence Bandarra's pronouncements dovetailed with the yearning for the return of Sebastian and he was proclaimed Sebastianism's prophet.

The final shape of the myth came in the seventeenth century from Father António Vieira, a Jesuit missionary who spent a great deal of time in Brazil. He was an implacable opponent of Protestant Holland, an orator and author of many beautifully-written sermons. Vieira held that Sebastian would return and lead the Portuguese again. He would take up the religious struggle towards the advent of the Fifth Empire, the Universal Empire of the Spirit, which would unite the Christians and the Jews and purify old sins. This final version of Sebastianism penetrated Portuguese literature, philosophy, art, folklore, and ever since has exerted a great influence in Portugal's spiritual life.

A great deal more can be said about the myth, and it is interpreted in different ways. It is usually at its strongest when the country is in a difficult political period. What is bizarre is that the hope of a return to greatness is built around the figure of the worst king that Portugal ever had. But he was mad and he strove for real greatness, and this is the kind of stuff from which myths are made.

Pessoa's interest in Sebastianism can be dated back to 1914 when, in a letter to an eminent philosopher of his day, known for his Sebastianist interests, he declares his intention to study the subject in depth. It thus overlaps precisely with the period when he was working on the poems of Campos, Caeiro and Reis. The myth had a real grip on Pessoa for long periods in his life. It fitted well with his attraction to the occult, to reincarnation, and it appealed to his sense of mission. Various manuscripts, later found amongst his writings, suggest that at times this was quite an obsession. He analysed past statesmen in order to see whether they were the incarnation of Sebastian. None of them were. So he aimed to establish the precise date of the king's return through numerological and astrological speculations. These speculations sometimes even led Pessoa to think that he himself maybe the new Sebastian. He commented on Bandarra's songs, projected writing a book on António Vieira. Sebastianism formed the base of his political convictions and, most of all, after the end of the Modernist experiments of *Orpheu* and *Portugal Futurista*, Sebastianism also began to inspire Pessoa the poet. In 1920 he published 'In Memory of the President-King Sidónio Pais'. In this poem the dictator, assassinated over a year earlier, is seen as another possible incarnation of Sebastian. Two years later Pessoa published a short cycle of patriotic poems *The Portuguese Sea* and there we find a poem to King Sebastian, 'Rise in the sun in me, and end the mist'.

It was not, however, that Pessoa simply shifted his attention away from the experiments in Modernist poetry to Sebastianism. What followed was a period when he seemed to be going in all sorts of directions. He was an intense patriot but he also wanted to be recognized as an English poet and brought out two volumes of poems that he had been writing since his time in South Africa. These included Shakespearean-style sonnets, and some erotic verse. Not a success. The English at best sounds quaint and the poems do not convince. He continued writing them almost until his death and right to the end he rated this output highly. He also tried his hand at French poetry but this he himself later dismissed as a mistake. Another oddity. In 1922, in the review *Contemporanea* he published *The Anarchist Banker*, a prose piece, which appears to have served to outline his political thinking. Two old friends meet in a restaurant. One of them, an ex-anarchist turned banker, explains his brand of individual anarchism. Through amassing a fortune, by means not always honest, he has liberated himself from the symbol of money, the most potent symbol of the bourgeois society. This way, he argues, he is more true to the anarchist principles than his old comrades. A somewhat perverse offering and why Pessoa should go ahead with its publication is something of a puzzle.

All this activity but for several years there was not a word from any of the fictional poets who mattered so much to Pessoa.

The first sign of new life came from Álvaro de Campos who published 'Lisbon Revisited 1923'. The following year Pessoa was involved in a new publishing venture, the literary review *Athena*, and it was there that he introduced the odes of Ricardo Reis and the following year a selection from Alberto Caeiro's *The Keeper of Flocks* and some other of his poems. *Athena* folded after five issues. Thereafter Pessoa collaborated with several reviews, most regularly with *Presença*, which represented what is referred to as the Second Portuguese Modernism. The great poems that come from this period are Campos's 'Lisbon Revisited 1926', 'The Tobacco Shop', and the extraordinary, blasphemous eighth poem from Caeiro's *The Keeper of Flocks*. A steady trickle of work by Reis and by Pessoa under his own name also appeared, amongst them the celebrated 'The poet is a feigner'.

In 1928 there is another bout of Sebastianist politics. In the same *Acção, Órgão do Núcleo de Acção Nacional* where Pessoa put out 'In Memory of the President-King Sidónio Pais', he publishes the infamous 'The Interregnum. Defence and Justification of Military Dictatorship', an ugly and unpalatable pamphlet, riddled with Sebastianist rhetoric.

In the early thirties Pessoa was again working intensely on Campos, Reis and Caeiro. Manuscripts show that he was preparing an introduction of which there are several versions. The one that came out was Campos's 'Recollections of my Master Caeiro'. The editors of *Presença* were repeatedly asking for more poems. At one point Pessoa promised the full version of Caeiro's *The Keeper of Flocks*; that was the work he was particularly proud of. He wrote in a letter that it was ready and that he was about to send it. He never did; completely out of step with character, Pessoa broke his promise. Instead, he was putting the finishing touches to a new cycle of poems. At first it was to be entitled *Portugal* but came out, in 1934, as *Message*.

Message is Pessoa's great Sebastianist work. It is a collection of 44 poems written over many years. The earliest dates from

1913, all but one of the poems from the earlier cycle *Portuguese Sea* were included, and most of the remainder were written in the few years preceding publication. They are usually short and tight, all written in rhythmic and rhyming stanzas. They have a vocabulary of great simplicity and economy, giving the whole construction a certain hermetic feel. The poems are arranged in three parts. The first two survey the country's golden past, its distinguished early royalty and the heroes of the great discoveries. The third part, entitled 'The Hidden One', is were the Sebastianist message is delivered—the past greatness is only a preparation for the future glory of the Fifth Empire embodied in the return of King Sebastian. And so there are poems to the King, a poem about the Fifth Empire, and in the section entitled 'Warnings', which consists of three poems, Pessoa traces a lineage of prophets. The first is 'Bandarra' ('Confused like the Universe/ And plebeian like Jesus Christ'), the second 'António Vieira' ('Emperor of the Portuguese tongue, but more/ He was the sky for us') and 'Third', Pessoa himself, ('By the waters of heartbreak I write this book'). The closing poem ends with a confident 'Comes the Hour'. Pessoa was persuaded to submit *Message* to a competition of poetry on a patriotic theme organized by the Secretariat for National Propaganda. It won the second prize, the first prize having been awarded to some absurd anti-communist poem that no-one now reads. It was the only time that Pessoa made money from his poetry.

Message is a Sebastianist poem through and through, but it also echoes Camões. The heraldry, which takes up the first two parts, is reminiscent of what we find in *The Lusiads*. Likewise, *Message* is about the conquest of the sea and here the reference is explicit—the monster Adamastor who bars da Gama's way around the Cape of Good Hope in *The Lusiads* also appears in *Message* under the name of Mostrengo. But rather strangely, although Pessoa honoured all the great figures of the past, and although he included a poem to the sea monster, Camões is absent. After reflecting on this for a moment, one realizes that Pessoa was right. Camões does not belong there. On account of the crusading streak that at times comes through in *The Lusiads*, many of the Sebastianists tend to include Camões in the tradition of the myth. But this is to strip him of everything he seems to have stood for. Camões was a learned humanist, a classicist, a man steeped in the tradition of the Renaissance. Sebastianism has its roots in folly and religious obscurantism. In its bare essentials it is an ideology of imperialism and colonialism. King Sebastian himself had little time for the humanities—it was to him that Camões dedicated, in vain, his epic.

Two of Pessoa's key works, the early 'Maritime Ode' and late *Message*, are an engagement with Camões. The responses could not be more different. Álvaro de Campos is a Modernist, and in 'Maritime Ode' he sets out to destroy the beautiful myth of *The Lusiads*. Campos has the destructiveness of an iconoclast who attacks to create a new poetic space. *Message* evokes the domain of Camões to expound a political myth. During the years that separate 'Maritime Ode' and *Message* Pessoa went through a constant vacillation between the poetic mission of bringing to the Portuguese a supra-Camões, on the one hand, and the essentially political and mystical call of Sebastianism, on the other. So when we view Pessoa's archipelago, the different personae, names, genres, languages, scattered around like isles and islets, we can discern two distinct groupings. The first is where we find Caeiro, Campos, Reis and parts of Pessoa himself. They are the grandchildren of Camões; they are the Modernist Pessoa. The second point of gravity centres round Sebastianism, occult and politics.

Camões and Sebastianism accompanied Pessoa for most of his literary life and, from the very beginning, there is a confusion. The terms in which he made his Supra-Camões statement already bear this out: 'One can argue that the current political movement is not of a type to produce supreme poetic geniuses. But *it is precisely for that reason* that we arrive more easily at the conclusion that a Supra-Camões will arrive in our land'. The curious thing about it is that, throughout Portugal's history, political decadence had nourished the longing for the lost king, not the poet. But historically Camões and Sebastian overlap precisely. When Camões was writing *The Lusiads* the country had just expelled the Jews and King Sebastian was setting out to Alcazar Kebir to fight the Arabs, the epic was dedicated to the King and Camões died the same year the country lost its independence as a result of Sebastian's adventure. These pivotal points of the country's past converge in Pessoa. They were alive in him, fashioning his thought, carving out his destiny. He suffered his country's demise and dreamed of a return to greatness. As a poet he aspired to the greatness of Camões but often sought his inspiration in Sebastian's mission.

Pessoa belonged to the voices of new poetic visions that were emerging in Europe, to those whose art was breaking the chains of history and also to those who were at the same time caught up in this very history's virulence. The tension between the poetic and the political calling was immense. It was enacted in Portuguese terms—Camões and Sebastianism—but it is a kind of tension that bears resemblance to what seemed quite common to other Modernist poets. Sebastianism may be very much a Portuguese phenomenon, but it bears traits which are at times not dissimilar to other ideologies brewing in Europe. It is similar because its roots are the same. The myth of the one Universal Faith led by chosen warriors is part of Europe's identity that was shaped in confrontation with the infidels. It goes back to the Crusades against the Arabs, to the expulsions of the Jews. In fact it is older than that. But before we get carried away with comparisons, one crucial point must be pointed out: Sebastianism never degenerated into a racist ideology, maybe because Bandarra, the first prophet, was a converted Jew; perhaps there are some other reasons. Its basic thrust was always messianic and it has often attracted enlightened individuals who gave it a spiritual meaning. Pessoa's Sebastianism was mostly of that type, a mystical yearning for an Empire of spiritual and artistic renewal. Yet there were also moments when his Sebastianism had very much a political, and even belligerent flavour. France

32

and Germany need to be militarily destroyed, thought Pessoa at one point. The last poem he seems to have finished and prepared for publication was 'Fifth Empire', an unabashed call to the Portuguese to show their superiority, and—to the tune of a bugle—conquer the world for a better future. But Pessoa never engaged in any propaganda activities; he never harboured any anti-Semitic feelings; his Futurist proclamations did not have the misogynist and warmongering drivel so characteristic of Marinetti's outbursts; he never served the State. He was not afraid of it either. When Salazar's *New State* began to home in on the Masonic organization, Pessoa went public in defence of Masonry. He apparently had no liking for Salazar, and in an autobiographical note that he prepared at the end of his life, he rejected 'Interregnum, Defence and Justification of Military Dictatorship' as a mistake. In the same autobiographical note Pessoa described his political position as 'Conservative in an English way, that is, liberal within the conservative frame, and resolutely anti-reactionary'. The description of his social position is laconic and a little chilling: 'anti-communist and anti-socialist. The rest follows from it'. Pessoa was naturally drawn to monarchy, had little faith in the democratic system, and often felt in step with dictatorial ideologies. But no state ever pleased him, and it never could, maybe because there was always the other Pessoa around, the poet who needed free air to breathe.

Sometimes the poet would desert Pessoa completely. At those moments he would write 'The Interregnum'; at other moments the poet and the political ideologist would join together and come up with a poem in which an assassinated president shines as the nation's saviour; then at times the poet would express a complete lack of respect for politicians. Here is a poem, not a great one, but interesting in this context. This closely rhyming (in the original) three-stanza poem is typical of the output that came under Pessoa's own name, but in this instance it was attributed to Álvaro de Campos. Pessoa published it a few months after 'Interregnum'.

Babylon's Lloyd Georges left
No trace on history.
Briands of Assyria or Egypt,
Trotskys of some Greek
Or Roman colony gone by—
All dead names, even written.

Only foolish poets, madmen
Who made their philosophies,
And judicious old geometrists
Have survived that anterior,
Miniscule darkness—
Even history's not history.

Oh great men of the Moment!
Oh great seething glories
Obscurity flees!
Take it all unthinking!
Pad your fame and bellies—
Tomorrow's for the madmen of today

And there was one more unusual thing about Pessoa. Many of the artists who held strong political or ideological views tended to keep them separate from their art. (This is less true of the artists from the left of the political spectrum as the revolutionary ideology, at least at the beginning, was sympathetic to the new artistic trends. Later, after the Stalinist order set in, it all became horribly complicated). Pessoa was different and more complex. For most of the time his work followed separate paths as though he was aware that between his political convictions and his artistic leanings there was an irreconcilable conflict, that there was no passage between one and the other. But he also sought to bring them together. He attempted this through transforming Camões into a Sebastianist message. This was his great undertaking of *Message*. The work certainly has poetic power; but in order to keep the message coherent, Camões had to be excluded.

In the last two or three years before his death Pessoa started seriously thinking of organising his writings for publication. The exact order in which he would bring them out is not all that clear as at different times he considered different schemes. But some rough plan emerges. First he would publish *Message*; this he would follow with writings that were either not yet ready (*The Book of Disquiet* or an English translation of *The Anarchist Banker*), or not at all written (a detective story), and then possibly the complete versions of Campos, Caeiro and Reis. In one letter he says that the poetry of these three would only come out after he had been awarded the Nobel Prize. A joke obviously, but that he had no plans for their imminent publication, though they were ready, is clear. Right to the end, poems of Campos and Reis were written, right to the end Pessoa thought of Caeiro's *The Keeper of Flocks* as one of his finest achievements, and yet he kept holding them back. One gets the impression that *Message* was meant to be the last word, the last port of call for a voyage that began with 'Maritime Ode'. And, being the last word, it was meant to submerge the others. This is how it looks. But this is not quite how it turned out. After publishing *Message* Pessoa explained in a letter that he was a 'national mystic', a 'rational Sebastianist' and then added: 'but I am also, mostly and often in contradiction to this, a lot of other things'. These other things were first and foremost the three imaginary companions: Alberto Caeiro, Ricardo Reis and Álvaro de Campos. Perhaps Pessoa knew all along that his greatness was in their verses, not in his Sebastianist mission. It may well be that he had some premonition of his impending death, that he knew that he would not be able to see his literary project through. Or maybe he knew that while alive he would never feel free enough, free from the curse of a Mission, to really let loose Caeiro and the others. One entertains such thoughts because, although Pessoa professed to have little intention of publishing them, there is every good reason to think that he made sure that they would get maximum posthumous exposure.

II

But if I want to say I exist as an entity that addresses and acts on itself, exercising the divine function of self-creation, then I'll make *to be* into a transitive verb. Triumphantly and anti-grammatically supreme, I'll speak of 'amming myself'.

The Book of Disquiet

During the years immediately after Pessoa's death, the public image of the poet was quite simple: author of *Message*, a great patriot with strong mystical leanings. Those who wanted to come to terms with this mysterious poet were studying the occult, Sebastianism and the like. The poems of Caeiro, Reis and Campos, scattered throughout various reviews and not easily available, were relatively little known. This changed when the critic João Gaspar Simões and the poet Luís de Montalvor, brought out in book form complete (at that time) editions of Caeiro & Co., as well as of the other poems that Pessoa wrote in his own name. These included all that Pessoa had published himself plus the many more found in his papers. More was discovered later yet these first editions were sufficient to bring home the immensity of Pessoa's imaginative power. Campos, Reis and Caeiro were not some subsidiary pseudonyms but a vast work, which in terms of volume dwarfs Pessoa's Sebastianism. After all, there were only three Sebastianist poems, some occult ones while the others were very prolific, and what they wrote turned out to be a real feast. Soon this strange theatre of fictional poets was recognized as Pessoa's major achievement. He invented it and exhausted it. To do it again, without being accused of plagiarism, would require prodigious poetic inventiveness.

Another thing. Contradicting the impression that he wanted to suppress this work, Pessoa left some instructions concerning the publication of these poets. He also wrote a letter to a young poet, Adolfo Casais Monteiro, describing how he came to invent them. The letter is long and goes into considerable detail. Pessoa begins with a psychiatric explanation and he ventures into a diagnosis: the multiple personality is a sign of a psycho-neurasthenia and it was to this that he ascribed his imaginary production. This psychological disturbance, he went on to say, was already manifest in early childhood. It began when he was six and remained with him ever since. And then at one point came Pessoa's stunning poetic coup: in virtually one go he transformed his inner multiple reality into a poetic strategy—the three new personalities, Alberto Caeiro, Ricardo Reis and Álvaro de Campos, emerged to accompany him for the rest of his literary life. Pessoa continues his letter with a description of the build-up to this momentous event:

Some time around 1912, unless I am mistaken (which couldn't be very much), the idea came to me to write some poems of a pagan character. I tried sketching some things in free verse (not in the style of Álvaro de Campos but in a semi-regular style), and then abandoned the attempt. But in the dim confusion I made a hazy outline of the person I was writing. (Without my knowing it, Ricardo Reis had been born). A year and a half or two later, I thought of playing a joke on Sá-Carneiro, inventing a bucolic poet, of a complicated sort, and presenting him, I don't recall now how, as though he were really a living creature. I spent a few days working on him but got nowhere. One day, just as I had finally given up—it was the 8th of March—I went over to a high desk and, taking a sheet of paper, began to write, standing, as I always write when I can. And I wrote thirty-odd poems straight off, in a kind of ecstasy whose nature I cannot define. It was the triumphal day of my life, and I shall never be able to have another like it. I started with a title—*The Keeper of Flocks*. And what followed was an apparition of somebody in me, to whom I immediately gave the name Alberto Caeiro. Forgive me the absurdity of the phrase: my master had appeared in me. This was my immediate sensation. As soon as I had written these thirty-odd poems I took another sheet of paper and wrote, also straight off, the six poems that make up Fernando Pessoa's *Oblique Rain*. Straight away and completely . . . It was the return of Fernando Pessoa-Alberto Caeiro to Fernando Pessoa himself alone; it was the reaction of Fernando Pessoa against his non-existence as Alberto Caeiro.

Alberto Caeiro having appeared, I sat down—instinctively and unconsciously—to give him disciples. I jerked the latent Ricardo Reis out of his false paganism, discovered his name, and adjusted him to himself, because at this stage I already *saw* him. And suddenly, in a derivation opposed to that of Ricardo Reis, there arouse in me impetuously a new individual. At one go, without interruption or correction, there arose the 'Triumphal Ode' of Álvaro de Campos—the Ode along with this name and the man along with the name he has.

This is an extraordinary, beguiling and very famous letter. It has everything in it. There is a psychopathological study which follows the classical psychiatric structure—first the diagnosis, then description of childhood symptoms, and in the end the full outbreak; there are touches of the supranatural—these poets 'appear' in him; most of all, there is myth-making. If anyone ever wondered how it is possible to write in one night first thirty-odd poems, then another six and to finish with a huge sprawling ode, the answer is that perhaps it is possible, but that Pessoa did not. The examination of the manuscripts carried out some years ago showed that they were written on different sittings although there is no doubt that they come from a short period of very intense activity. Pessoa was using this letter to shape his posthumous mythology, further contradicting the impression that he wanted *Message* to be his last word. The letter seemed to be a way of preparing the ground for the final presentation of the poets as Pessoa made it plain that he expected it to be published. Monteiro duly did. The 8th of March 1914 may now be recognized as a mythological date but it has already entered the folklore of literature. 'I desire to be a creator of myths, which is the highest mystery that any human being can perform'. Pessoa's ploy was a success.

These imaginary personae were not a disguise, an attempt to conceal the author, the way a pseudonym would. At any rate, it was known in literary circles right from the beginning that Pessoa was behind them. Campos, Reis and Caeiro were *other* poets, other from the author as King Lear is other than Shakespeare, to use Pessoa's favourite example. He called them heteronyms, a word he seems to have coined.

Seventy-two names have been found in Pessoa papers. Sometimes they are referred to as seventy-two heteronyms, or potential heteronyms. Some of them were quite developed, others only popped up for a short spell. Caeiro, Campos and Reis were different and in the end only they should be referred to as heteronyms. They were the only ones who gained full poetic coherence and independence. But it is not only the fact that they were more developed that distinguishes them from the others, there was another important difference. They emerged when Pessoa was in his most exciting period. It was 1914 and Pessoa was part of a group who set up the literary magazine *Orpheu*. The other principal members were Mario de Sá-Carneiro—a close friend of Pessoa with whom he had a strong poetic affinity; José de Almada Negreiros—a poet, pamphleteer and painter, irreverent to the extreme, sometimes hysterically funny; Santa Rita-Pintor—a painter who noisily espoused Futurism; Armando Côrtes-Rodrigues—a poet from the Azores; Luís de Montalvor—another poet who had been a diplomat in Brazil and was to provide a link with the overseas Portuguese speaking constituency; Amadeo de Souza-Cardoso—a painter who joined the group a little later and who was one of the most outstanding: had he not died so young he would have become one of the great European artists, a loss on a par with that of Gaudier Brzeska. There were others. The group was a mixed bag. Some of the members were tortured souls (one of the contributors to the second issue of *Orpheu* was an actual inmate in a psychiatric hospital) but they had things in common: they were all gifted and they wanted to introduce new art to the stale and provincial Portuguese scene.

They enjoyed scandalising the public and *Orpheu* was in this respect a great success. The response, some of it coming from leading newspapers, was of outrage. These artists were mad, that was the general opinion, they should all be in a hospital, together with the one contributor who was already there, a fact many of the reviewers did not fail to exploit. Pessoa enjoyed the noise. He wrote in a letter, with evident pleasure, 'the scandal is enormous. In the street fingers are pointed at us. Everyone—even outside literature—is talking about *Orpheu*'. *Orpheu* became the high point of Portuguese Modernism. Its influence was enormous, although the adventure did not last long. After two issues it closed because of financial problems.

The birth of the heteronyms had much to do with *Orpheu*. The whole affair began when Pessoa decided to play a joke on Sá-Carneiro and invent a bucolic poet—this is at least how Pessoa tells the story. He came up with three poets who, in a sense, were as much members of *Orpheu* as the others. Campos published straight away in the periodical and his poems were part of its success. The poems of Caeiro and Reis, although at that time not published, were also well known to the other members of the group. The heteronyms were part of a human milieu, the *Orpheu* group were their companions. The other fictional personae that were later discovered in Pessoa's trunk remained unknown actors in his inner theatre.

Orpheu was a time of exuberance that really infected Pessoa. Of the many notes in his manuscripts the writings about this period are the most alive. In fact, comparing them with his commentaries on Bandarra and Vieira is like comparing a carnival with a funeral march. And then tragedy struck. Sá-Carneiro committed suicide. That was 1916. Two years later Spanish influenza cut down the painters Santa Rita-Pintor and Souza-Cardoso; others left town. Pessoa was lonely, and so were Campos, Caeiro and Reis. They fell silent. It took them quite some time to return to life and later they owed much to the interest of Gaspar Simões and Casais Monteiro, a critic and poet from the next generation.

Any attempt to reconstruct the true genesis of the heteronyms is doomed to failure. Pessoa covered his tracks. But it does not matter. Any 'truth' about it would be far more prosaic than the myth that he left behind. And it has a very clear logic of its own. Alberto Caeiro was the first to emerge and he apparently appeared from nowhere. His poems come in three parts: *The Keeper of Flocks*, eight poems of *The Shepherd in Love* and seventy-odd *Detached Poems*. *The Keeper of Flocks* is one of Pessoa's most accomplished works. It is a cycle of 49 poems which, when read in one sitting, unfold like a small treatise. What they have to say is simple: the only reality comes from the senses. To begin with, Caeiro has no need of God,

> I don't believe in God because I never saw him.
> If he wanted me to believe in him,
> I have no doubt he'd come talk with me
> (. . . . . .)
>
> But if God is the flowers and the trees
> And the hills and the sun and the moonlight,
> Then I believe in him
> (. . . . . .)
>
> But if God is the trees and the flowers
> And the hills and the moonlight and the sun,
> Why should I call him God? (V)

But it is not only God, all other inventions of the civilized mind—metaphysics, religion, names—are a source of confusion and unhappiness. 'Metaphysics? What metaphysics do those trees have?' (V), 'Things don't have meaning—they only have existence' (XXXIX).

> But things don't have a name or a personality:
> They exist, and the sky is big and the earth is wide,
> And our heart is the size of a clenched fist . . . (XXVII)

In order to deliver his teaching Caeiro writes in the simplest of free verses, without the guardrail of rhyme and metre. His poems speak about nature and he wants them to flow as naturally as a stream, and to be enjoyed like a stream. 'I don't bother with Rhyme. Two trees / Are never, ever the same, one beside the other' (XIV). According to one commentary, written in English by a certain Thomas Crosse—another of Pessoa's heteronyms—Caeiro is 'a poet of what may be called "the absolute Concrete" he never looks on that concrete *otherwise than abstractly*. No man is more sure of the absolute, non-subjective reality of a tree, of a stone, of a flower. Here it might be thought that he would particularize, that he would say an "oak", a "sacred stone", a "marigold". But he does not: he keeps on saying a "tree", a "stone", a "flower"'. Caeiro's vocabulary is stripped to the bare minimum. It is as though senses only corresponded to basic words but not to names. And consequently, through repeating that a flower is a flower, a tree is a tree, Caeiro sometimes slips into a monotonous tautology.

Caeiro does not seem credible. Why would he write? How can he write and live by the senses? This is incongruous. But somehow Caeiro is believable. Perhaps because he does not quite live by the senses but only strives to, surrounded by the modern world. And he is not immune: 'Yes, even I, who live only on living, / Men's lies come to meet me' (XXVI). There are also four poems (XV–XVIII) where Caeiro is not well and feels the opposite of what he is. He would like to be something else, just a mere inanimate object, which '. . . would be better than going through life / Looking back and feeling sorry about it . . .' (XVIII). But, perhaps most of all, we listen to Caeiro because he teaches. In the second poem he declares: 'I don't have a philosophy: I have senses . . .'. This is true only in part. Caeiro develops a philosophy of non-philosophy that demands 'The main thing is knowing how to see / To know how to see without thinking' (XXIV). What he has to say deserves to be called a philosophy because of its consistency and because this unlearning is indeed very thorough. It runs on several levels. It begins with the basics from which modern thinking evolves—metaphysics and God. Then Caeiro proceeds to dismantle concepts that issue from them. Almost every poem enters the conflict between Caeiro's gaze—pagan and pure, and the poisoned civilized mind. The list is quite long and comprehensive. He rejects memory (XLIII), geography and history (XX), time (XLIV). These notions link appearances, they give them meaning and significance beyond what they are. Caeiro, the pagan, cannot accept this; he is the Nature poet. And in these marvellous lines, coming from one of the *Detached Poems*, he slams the back door through which some form of pantheism, for many the favoured mix of innocence and religion, could sneak in:

> Sometimes I start looking at a stone.
> I don't start thinking if it feels.
> I don't lose myself and call it my sister.
> But I like it because it's being a stone,
> I like it because it doesn't feel anything,
> I like it because it doesn't have any kinship with me.

What may have at first seemed a simple teaching turns out to be quite radical, full of nuance and subtlety. This is why, despite such economy of means, *The Keeper of Flocks* is so compelling. It is poetry of the surface where the only thing that counts is appearance with nothing hidden.

> I'm the Discoverer of Nature.
> I'm the Argonaut of true sensations.
> I bring a new Universe to the Universe
> Because I bring the Universe itself. (XLVI)

One poem stands out—the eighth. Pessoa at first withheld it because he did not want to offend the Catholic friend who was running *Athena*, which is where Caeiro's poems first appeared. Of all the work published during his life this is Pessoa's strongest anti-Catholic statement. The scorn with which he treats the official doctrine is extraordinary and some of the lines are really unforgettable. The Virgin Mary?—'She wasn't even a woman: she was [a] handbag'. And then:

> The Virgin Mary spends her afternoons in eternity knitting socks.
> The Holy Ghost picks at himself with his beak
> And perches on armchairs and dirties them.
> Everything in heaven is as stupid as the Catholic Church.

It may appear strange that the quiet and peaceful Caeiro is given the task of venting Pessoa's anti-Church feelings. But it is Caeiro who delivers himself of such thoughts because the Church's doctrine is rejected in the name of the innocence of sensationism—God is not a man who suffers for mankind on a cross, he is a child who feels and laughs and rolls in the grass. Childhood is the divine state; whatever we retain from childhood is what is godly in us.

> And it's because he's always with me that I'm always a poet,
> And my very smallest glimpse
> Fills me with feeling,
> And the smallest sound, whatever it may be,
> Seems to speak to me.

Caeiro blasphemes in search of the innocence of childhood. Many poets have sought to recover this state. To some this is nostalgia for a time that is no longer, to others it may be the lost mother, to others still, the ability to imagine and mythologize without restraint. Caeiro's child is a being that has only senses and to whom each vision is the wonder of the new. This is the state of grace. The whole poem is a coming together of blasphemy and innocence shaping some of the most tender images in all of Pessoa's poetry:

> The New Child who stays where I stay
> Gives one hand to me
> And the other to everything that exists
> And so we three go along whatever road there is . . .

Caeiro was the first of Pessoa to be translated into English and the circumstances were not usual. The translator was Thomas Merton, the American Trappist monk who later in his life became attracted to Eastern religions. He found in Caeiro a Zen sensibility and translated a dozen poems from *The Keeper of Flocks* to show to Daisetsu Suzuki, the great exponent of Buddhism in the West, that in Europe there was also a Zen poet. Since then the notion of Caeiro the Zen poet has been quite often repeated. One can easily see what made Merton regard Caeiro this way. A certain calm and quiet wonder of the everyday ordinariness that comes through in these poems is so un-Western and so reminiscent of the Eastern mentality that the comparison is quite natural. There are also odd two-liners that would comfortably sit in an anthology of Buddhist poetry. But this is more or less where the similarity ends. A comparison with Basho, for example, would only show great differences. If nothing else Caeiro's tone is too often too polemical to pass for a Zen poet. Pessoa himself, although he had a fair idea of what Buddhism stood for, never made the slightest suggestion that Caeiro represented anything of the sort. He was proud to have created a poet who seemed so different. In the many introductions he wrote, when he was planning to launch Caeiro, he liked to stress that in our world the purity of Caeiro's gaze is a marvel and that this is because they come from a real pagan sensibility. And *The Keeper of Flocks* may have been written in a few bursts, the persona of Caeiro may have appeared to Pessoa from nowhere, but the scope of Caeiro's argument, its coherence and consistence, indicate that Pessoa put into these poems a great deal of philosophical thought which he had been mulling over for quite some time. Almost every poem nibbles away at some issue, making an additional point, completing the argument. Going through Pessoa's notes on philosophy one can see the kind of preparatory work that he had done. He spent a great deal of time studying the early Greeks. It is interesting that Campos describes Caeiro in his 'Recollections of my Master Caeiro' as Greek-like, his mind not poisoned by the idea of infinity. Somewhere in these pre-Christian thinkers that Pessoa studied are the many thoughts that we find in *The Keeper of Flocks*, although there does not seem to be any early programme that was already prepared and then put into these verses. It looks that it all came together—as often in dramatic invention—only after the persona of Caeiro emerged.

But Merton had a point. He draws attention to a certain mood of Caeiro's poems, though it is not always evoked by Zen-like lines. These, opening poem XXXVII, are as good as anything coming from the Imagists:

> Like a great big blob of dirty fire
> The setting sun lags among left-over clouds.
> A vague whistle comes from far away in the very calm
>   evening.
> There must be a train out there.

In the penultimate poem Caeiro speaks of his poems as though they were flowers on the tree, and just as the tree cannot hide its flowers so he has to give his verses to all to read. The final poem ends the day. Caeiro closes the door, lights the lamp and reposes:

> Without reading anything, or thinking about anything, or
>   even sleeping,
> A feel of life running through me like a river along its bed,
> And outside a silence as big as a sleeping god.

It is not surprising that Pessoa was always proud of this creation.

Pessoa said in the letter that the emergence of Alberto Caeiro meant the non-existence of Fernando Pessoa. This makes perfect sense. Caeiro, the sensationist poet, is the antithesis of Pessoa, the Sebastianist with mystical leanings. There is an unbridgeable gap between the doctrine of sensationism and the occult, which seeks meaning beyond the visible. It is not only something that we can infer: there are also a few lines that sound like direct jibes at this Pessoa—'the only occult meaning of things / Is that they have no occult meaning at all' (XXXIX), and in another poem: 'Mystical poets are sick philosophers / And philosophers are crazy' (XXVIII). What is Pessoa's response? He does not counter, so to speak, with an occult poem but instead he writes a cycle of six poems *Oblique Rain*, which launched a short-lived movement called 'intersectionism'. These poems are an attempt to develop a form of poetic cubism. Different parallel sensations are laid out next to each other, blurred, obscured; dream and reality, the external and the internal are brought together, mingled and deliberately confused. Later he went on to abandon intersectionism and the earlier 'isms' which he had tried to develop, but one thing remained: on the 8th of March 1914, together with Caeiro, Reis and Campos, a new Pessoa was born. He came after Caeiro and he always considered Caeiro his master. It is from him that he learned the wisdom of the senses. How can this post-Caeiro Pessoa be defined? Which are the poems that are written by him and which by the other Pessoa?

> But in the beginning was the Word, occluded
> Here when the Infinite Light, now snuffed,
> Was brought from Chaos, ground of Being, and fed
> To the Shadow, and the absent Word was clouded.
>
> Yet if the Soul perceives her own form blundered
> In herself, which is Shadow, she at least sees, splendid,
> The Word of this World, human and anointed,
> Perfect Rose that in God is crucified.
>
> Then we, lords of the thresholds of the Skies,
> Can go searching beyond God to surprise
> The Master's secret and the profound Good;
>
> Not from here only, from us now, aroused,
> Freed at last in the actual blood of Christ
> From the World's generation—its death to God.

This is the middle sonnet of one of Pessoa's great occult poems 'At the Tomb of Christian Rosenkreuz'. To follow the spirit of the letter, this poem, as well as the other occult poems, should be seen as separate from the work of the post-Caeiro Pessoa. But Pessoa himself did not always see it this way. In the third edition of *Orpheu*, which never appeared, he intended to publish a series of occult poems entitled *Beyond God*. The fact that he planned to bring them out in *Orpheu*, not some other review, does not square with the idea of the post-Caeiro Modernist Pessoa who would have nothing to do with the occult. Also, when he thought of a comprehensive edition of his poetry he did not consider keeping the occult poems apart, either. And this is how Pessoa is usually published. Only the Sebastianist poems are presented in a different section, the rest of Pessoa's verse comes together under the general title *Songbook*. But perhaps right at the end Pessoa changed his mind. In the letter to Casais Monteiro about the genesis of the heteronyms he also wrote a long passage about his occult beliefs. Pessoa authorized the publication of the letter under the strict condition that these revelations be suppressed. (Monteiro at first respected Pessoa's wish and the suppressed part became known only some fifteen years later.) This suggests that when he was finally preparing the presentation of Caeiro, Reis and Campos—in which the publication of this letter was to play a role—he wanted to keep the occult away from the heteronyms.

So it seems that in order to arrive at some defined picture of the post-Caeiro Pessoa we can legitimately disregard the occult as well as the Sebastianist poems. We then discover that the rest does not present us with any clear image. All of the poems are carefully crafted with attentiveness to rhyme and rhythm (as are the Sebastianist and occult ones), but otherwise there is no particular dominant theme, and the poems vary from one to another. We find some love poems, some which give the sense of a yearning—to be someone else, for a home that never was. Often there are images of women; in one of them the poet is moved by a harvestwoman's song. One poem

'We Took the Town After an Intense Bombardment' with its image of a child lying dead on the road with his guts spilling out reads like an anti-war statement, not a frequent theme in Pessoa's work. These are usually short poems that catch a fleeting sensation, or an image that touches something deeper. If there is any influence of Caeiro it is that they usually begin with an image, something quite tactile, though not by any means always. Throughout this varied output the feelings that are most frequent are melancholy and sadness. But just as one thinks that a certain prevailing mood underlines these verses, Pessoa writes some late poems that undermine any attempt to attribute these feelings to him. Feelings cannot be grasped, anyway, 'Because feeling is like the sky— / Seen, nothing in it to see', and besides, all his feelings are imagined. Two poems deal with this precisely; the first is entitled 'This':

> They say I pretend or lie
> All I write. No such thing.
> It simply is that I
> Feel by imagining.
> I don't use the heart-string.
>
> All that I dream or lose,
> That falls short or dies on me,
> Is like a terrace which looks
> On another thing beyond.
> It's that thing leads me on.
>
> And so I write in the middle
> Of things not next one's feet,
> Free from my own muddle,
> Concerned for what is not.
> Feel? Let the reader feel!

In the other poem, 'Autopsychography', one of Pessoa's most famous, written a year earlier, we find that the relation between the poet, his feelings and those of the reader verges on the cynical:

The poet is a feigner.
So completely does he feign
that the pain he truly suffers
he even feigns as pain.

And those who read his writings
will feel the printed pain,
not the two that he has suffered
but the one that they will feign.

And so around its trackage
the little clockwork train
we call the heart, goes spinning
to entertain the brain.

The poet is the argonaut of imaginary sensations. He can feel anything; experience anything. He travels without leaving his armchair.

Although born together with Caeiro, Reis and Campos this Pessoa had a precursor. Some time earlier he had written a 'static drama', *The Mariner*, an interesting early work that has a special place in Pessoa's opus. It is indeed a 'static drama', more static than anything Beckett ever wrote. Throughout the play three women sit, doing nothing and saying virtually nothing. The only thing that comes near to animating them is a story of a sailor who is stranded on an uninhabited island and develops an imaginary life, richer than anything he has known before. It is here that Pessoa for the first time expounded his doctrine of the superiority of imaginary over real life. The review *Renascença*, where Pessoa had already published two poems, refused it. Pessoa was probably not aggrieved. By this time he was moving away from the review's symbolist leanings, as he had already met those with whom he was to set up *Orpheu*. *The Mariner* was published in *Orpheu* and Pessoa never collaborated with *Renascença* again.

After Caeiro and Pessoa came Ricardo Reis, 'jerked out of his false paganism', though what this exactly meant Pessoa did not explain. Reis is the least visible of the heteronyms. He did not write anything on that mythical day and he published little. Later it was discovered that his output was considerable. He was conservative in his tastes and modelled his poetry on Horace. The language of his verse was sophisticated, at times somewhat mannered, and the entire output came in the form of a tight, sometimes epigrammatic, free verse Ode. The first was written sometime in 1914 the last only two weeks before Pessoa's death in 1935. Throughout these twenty years the style remained the same and their subject rarely changed. Life is not worth living and there is nothing to look for beyond it. Our knowledge is limited and unequal to that of the gods. We must learn to appreciate the little that comes our way. If we expect much we will face disappointment, 'but to one who hopes for nothing/ All that comes is grateful.' Like the ancients, Reis believes in the gods but does not believe that they concern themselves with human affairs: 'on the calm Olympus / They are another Nature'. Resigned to fate, Reis dreams his unreal pagan world. He seeks to recreate the sensibility of Greece and Rome but none of their Dionysian pleasures. Living in a garden filled with roses and lilies, he sublimates his carnal yearnings into odes to nymph-like women—Lydia, Chloe, Neaera—passive, silent embodiments of pure spirit, just as unreal as the garden he lives in.

> I love the roses from the gardens of Adonis,
> Lydia, I love those volucrines, the roses,
>   For on the day they bloomed,
>   On that day they died.
> Light for them is eternal, since
> They bloomed after the sun rose, and died
>   Before Apollo left
>   His visible course.
> So let us make our life one day,
> Ignorant, Lydia, willfully,
>   Of the night surrounding
>   The little we last.

Pessoa referred to Reis as a sad Epicurean, but he is so sad that there is not much of Epicurus left. The only element that could be so named is Reis's view that the gods dwell away from human affairs. The rest has either nothing to do with Epicurus or is superficial. Epicurus did not believe in fate, to which Reis resigns himself; his Garden was a living community, the men and women that surrounded him were real, as were his pleasures, though more modest than some believe.

It seems that this spiritual suffering dressed in a classical idiom was for Pessoa an exercise in form. He was drawn to the old masters. In his English poems he attempted to produce a modern version of the Shakespearean sonnet. But Pessoa's English was no way near as mastered as he thought and his attempts to imitate Shakespeare could not be anything else but a failure. Reis is different. Here, the Latin Horace is re-worked into Portuguese, of which Pessoa was a master and the result was obviously different. The form is also tighter, which seemed to suit Pessoa better. At any rate, Reis kept at it, perfecting his craft, all his life.

All the odes are carefully constructed, though none really stand out as exceptional. Year after year, unhurriedly, Reis constructs his verse, spinning out new variations on a never changing theme. And just like Caeiro, who in the eighth poem of *The Keeper of Flocks* changes his tone, we find a few poems that disrupt the calm of Reis's ancient pantheon. The reason is exactly the same—he also harbours anti-Christian feelings.

> Hate you, Christ, I do not, or seek. I believe
> In you as in the other gods, your elders.
>   I count you as neither more nor less
>   Than they are, merely newer.
>
> I do hate, yes, and calmly abhor people
> Who seek you above the other gods, your equals.
>   I seek you were you are, not higher
>   Than them, not lower, yourself merely.

Sad god, needed perhaps because there was
None like you: one more in the Pantheon, nothing
  More, not purer: because the whole
  Was complete with gods, except you.

Take care, exclusive idolater of Christ: life
Is multiple, all days different from each other,
  And only as multiple shall we
  Be with reality and alone.

This, and the few other similar poems, only saw light after Pessoa's death. It was rare that he would make public his anti-Catholic feelings. Reis rejects the Christian God just as violently as Caeiro does, although the reasons are different. There is a discernible progression. Caeiro does not accept any deity, however conceived. He is a poet of innocence surrounded by fields where nothing is eternal. Reis is a sophisticated intellectual. Surrounded by garden walls he meditates on the lives of the unperturbed gods who are wise enough not to concern themselves with human affairs. He finds the Christian idolatry aggressive and it offends his sensitive soul. He also argues the same point that animated Pessoa and which Campos made a central issue in his 'Ultimatum'—we are multiple. It follows that as multiple we cannot accept a universe in which there is only one god. In his very last poem Reis speaks of this multiplicity in a striking form:

Legion live in us;
I think or feel and don't know
Who it is thinking, feeling.
I am merely the place
Where thinking or feeling is.

I have more souls than one.
There are more 'I's than myself.
And still I exist
Indifferent to all.
I silence them: I speak.

The crisscross thrusts
Of what I feel or don't feel
Dispute in the I I am.
Unknown. They dictate nothing
To the I I know. I write.

The pastoral Caeiro, Pessoa the feigner, Reis the Classicist
and then the last to emerge was Álvaro de Campos, Pessoa's
steadiest and at the same time most volatile companion. He
arose 'impetuously' with 'Triumphal Ode', a fitting title to end
what Pessoa called a triumphant day. Campos wrote a lot. From
the first early period come 'Maritime Ode', 'Opium Eater' and
the unfinished 'Absurd Hour' and 'Salute to Walt Whitman'.
The last two were only published posthumously. All of them,
except 'Opium Eater', were written in free verse, 'Salute to
Walt Whitman' makes the affinity clear. The other influence
was Marinetti, whose Futurist teachings reached Lisbon a few
years earlier and made a great impression on the *Orpheu* group.
Speed, machines, modernity attract Campos and he throws
himself into everything headlong.

In the painful light of big electric factory-lamps
I have a fever and I write.

Factory lamps and fever—thus opens 'Triumphal Ode'. And
later:

I could die ground up by a motor
With the delicious surrender felt by a woman possessed.
Hurl me into furnaces!
Shove me under trains!
Bludgeon me aboard ships!
Masochism through mechanism!
Sadism of whatever's modern and me and the clamour!

Some have seen in these lines traces of latent homosexuality.
Maybe. But Campos wants to experience everything—a sea

voyage of bygone days as well as modern technology. He is a poet who embraces all that modernity stands for: machines, drugs, alcohol, travel. His language is that of everyday speech, as it is spoken by vagrants, vagabonds, bums, pimps. He liked to keep their company.

> I love and animate everything, give humanity to everything,
> To men and stones, souls and machines,
> Enlarging my own personality by doing so.

> I belong to everything so as always to belong more to myself,
> And my ambition would be to carry the universe in my arms
> Like a child being kissed by its nurse.

Campos is exuberant. He feels particularly close to Whitman. They are soul brothers who sing a poetic hymn to the new humanity. He pays homage to Whitman with a long poem. 'Holding hands, Walt, holding hands, while the universe dances in our souls.' But the poem remains unfinished and it is one of the last that Campos will write for some time. When he takes up writing again he sounds different. He still writes in free verse but Whitman's exuberance is no longer there. He is depressed. In the three great poems of the later period 'Lisbon Revisited 1923', 'Lisbon Revisited 1926' and 'The Tobacco Shop' the pain is explicit. In the first of the two Lisbon poems Campos is feeling besieged by others, he is sick of all those who tell him who to be, who tell him about morals and aesthetics. 'Go to hell without me,/ Or let me go there by myself!'. The other poem is sadder and in it the loss of childhood comes through:

> Once again I see you, City of my childhood terrifyingly
>   lost . . .
> City of my sorrow and joy, I dream here again . . .
> I? But am I the same person who lived here once and
>   returned,
> And came back here again and again?

And now come back here again, am I?
Or are we, all the I's I was or were here,
A string of bead-beings strung all together by a memory
    strand,
A string of dreams of myself which someone outside me
    dreamt up?

'The Tobacco Shop', the most famous of Campos's poems of that period begins:

I'm nothing.
I'll never be anything.
I can't wish to be anything.
Even so, I have in me all the dreams of the world.

From this unpromising beginning Campos, sitting at the window and watching the street, weaves a meditation on the futility of his life; the two—the meditation and the view of the street—alternate. He moves from sadness to a melancholic pleasure coming from the sense of belonging, and in the unexpected conclusion Campos is touched by the ordinariness of what he sees, it takes him out of his sorry state. It is one of the most beautiful of all of Pessoa's poems. But as the years progressed a really desperate feeling would come into his verse. One of his last poems is particularly savage. No question, anymore, as he did earlier with Walt Whitman, of lovingly embracing the universe.

Not a minute too soon . . . this is perfect . . .
There it is!
There's my madness, right there in my head!

My heart exploded like a cardboard bomb
And sent shockwaves up my spine right into my brain . . .

Thank God I'm nuts!
Thank God everything I ever did came back to me as trash,
Like I was spitting in the wind,

And spattered all over my face!
That everything I ever was got tangled underfoot
Like excelsior for shipping precisely nothing!
That everything I ever thought is sticking its finger down my
    throat
And making me want to puke on an empty stomach!
Thank God, because, like being drunk,
This is a solution.
How do you like that . . . I found a solution, but I had to use
    my stomach!
I found a truth, I felt it in my guts!

Transcendental poetry — already done it!
Grand lyric rapture — strictly old hat!
Organizing various poems by decreasing vastness of subject —
No news at all.
I need to throw up, to throw up my self . . .
I'm so nauseated that if I could eat the universe just to spew it
    into the sink, I'd do it.
It'd be a struggle, but there'd be a purpose to it.
At least there'd be a purpose.
The way things are, I don't have a purpose, or even a life.

Campos' range is impressive. He is introvert and extrovert,
exuberant and depressed, he laughs and he moans; a sort of
manic-depressive. Fever, boredom, anguish are all spluttered
out with abandon. Campos may declare in a moment of
exasperation 'shit to all of humanity' but he is the most human
of the many poets that Pessoa was.

Thus we have a constellation of four poets—Caeiro is the naïve,
Pessoa the inventor, Reis a classicist and Campos is modern. Each
has his own technique, vocabulary and subject. The poetry of
each of them is very accessible. The experiences, thoughts and
feelings—imaginary or real—are of a kind we easily sense. In
other words, none of them has a poetic sensitivity that is hard to
enter and they do not present the kind of difficulties as Rimbaud,
or Mallarmé, for example, do. It is impressive that Pessoa could
create an oeuvre so rich out of a world so accessible through

means, which are so simple. Pessoa was in the technical sense a restrained poet and always remained within the canon. Even Campos's most futurist experiments were never as extravagant as those of some of his *Orpheu* companions, or of Apollinaire, to quote a more familiar example. He only went so far as to sometimes drop punctuation, add a few sound effects, put in an odd foreign word, or in 'Maritime Ode' an English poem. But that is all. The poems are always coherent, logical, written in stanzas, and they do not require any effort to disentangle their meaning. Literary references are almost altogether absent; even Reis's Odes, with their classicisms and ancient gods, can be read without the help of a dictionary of mythology. All this is very different from *The Waste Land*, for example, to which Eliot appended several pages of notes to elucidate the meaning of the poem; or from Yeats who often cannot be understood without familiarity with Irish history; or, for that matter, from Pessoa's *Message*, which likewise cannot be understood without familiarity with Portuguese history. Not only do these poems eschew erudition, they also virtually never have any relation to the 'real' world outside them, either. So while, taken as a whole, Pessoa is a very Portuguese phenomenon, the Caeiro-Pessoa-Reis-Campos quartet are outside history, outside tradition, and belong to no particular place. Their poetic universe is what they have created themselves. The images are of their own bar one or two exceptions, like Caeiro's child-God who appears earlier in the work of another Portuguese poet Teixeira de Pascoaes, or these lines from Wordsworth: 'A primrose by the river's brim / A yellow primrose was to him, / And it was nothing more', which Campos points out express the same sentiment as Caeiro's poems, although Caeiro could not have known them as he did not read English.

Right from the beginning Pessoa saw Caeiro, Campos and Reis as a group of real personalities. They were his 'coterie'. He supplied them with biographies, told us what they looked like. This is what he tells about them in the letter to Casais Monteiro:

I can *see* before me, in the colourless yet real space of a dream, the faces and the miens of Caeiro, Ricardo Reis and Álvaro de Campos. It was I who fabricated their ages and their lives. Ricardo Reis was born in 1887 (I cannot recall the exact day nor the month, but I do have them somewhere) in Oporto, is a doctor by profession and is at present in Brazil. Alberto Caeiro was born in 1889 and died in 1915. He was born in Lisbon but spent most of his life in the country. He did not have a profession or any real education to speak of. Álvaro de Campos was born in Tavira [Algarve] on October 15th 1890 (at 1.30pm, so I am told by Ferreira Gomes; and it is certainly true as his horoscope for this hour confirms.) As you know he is a naval engineer (from Glasgow) but is now here in Lisbon, but not working. Caeiro was of medium stature and although in fact of a very delicate disposition (he died of tuberculosis) he did not appear as delicate as he was. Ricardo Reis is slightly, though only slightly, smaller in stature, stronger but leaner. Álvaro de Campos is tall (1.75 metres—two centimetres taller than I), thin and a little inclined to stoop. They all have clean-shaven faces: Caeiro was fair, without much colour and blue eyes; Reis a vague opaque swarthy colour and Campos somewhere between white and brown resembling slightly a typical Portuguese Jew; his hair, however, is straight and is normally parted at the side, he wears a monocle. As I have said, Caeiro hardly received any education at all, only primary school. Both his father and mother died early in his life and he just carried on living at home, surviving on a small independent income. He lived with an old great-aunt. Ricardo Reis, educated in a Jesuit College, is, as I said, a doctor; he has been living in Brazil since 1919 when he chose to expatriate because he was a monarchist. He is a Latinist as a result of the education he received from others and a semi-Hellenist as a result of the education he gave himself. Álvaro de Campos had a typical secondary school education and later was sent to Scotland to study engineering. During one holiday period he undertook the journey to the Orient from which emerged 'Opium Eater'. He was taught Latin by an uncle, a priest, from the Beiras.

This is the longest description of the heteronyms that Pessoa gave and the only detail that escaped him, but is mentioned elsewhere, was that Caeiro spent the last months in Lisbon where he died. On the whole these biographies are no more than rough sketches. What is their purpose? They certainly do not elucidate anything about the poems, they do not make Caeiro & Co. any more believable—their verisimilitude is in their poetry. If the purpose of these biographies is not immediately clear than at least they are quite logical. First Caeiro. After his doctrine of the absolute reality of the senses had been expounded his task was completed. He came from nowhere and had nowhere to go. His short life is the short life of innocence. Then Reis. In Brazil, away from his literary companions, he can indulge in the ethereal meditation on the uselessness of life and in the re-working Horace. Campos, by contrast, is very present. He is around in Lisbon. He publishes poems regularly, he continues with pamphlets. He makes public some of his views concerning the others. He praises Caeiro; Pessoa's *The Mariner* bores him stiff. He could also be really insolent. One incident, very early on in the *Orpheu* period, even shocked some of his friends. A left-wing political leader, much detested by Pessoa, was almost killed in a tram accident. Campos wrote a letter to a newspaper commenting on the accident. He delighted in 'an hour so deliciously mechanical where divine providence itself uses trams for its high designs'. Campos was always liable to act in an unruly fashion. At one point he went so far as to interfere in Pessoa's one romantic affair, writing letters to the woman in question, Ophelia, advising her to leave Pessoa alone. Ophelia told Pessoa she did not like Campos one bit.

One apparent reason for creating the biographies, apart from giving the poets substance, was to dramatise the heteronymic strategy. Caeiro, Reis, Campos and Pessoa himself were meant as a group and not just a collection of individuals. They knew each other, though their biographies made their direct contact limited. Caeiro was dead by 1915, Reis left for Brazil four years later. But they had met; they knew each other's work, commented on it and were together engaged in creating a new artistic and philosophical paganism. There was also a certain António Mora. He wrote two masterpieces: *The Return of the Gods* and *Prolegomena for the Reformation of Paganism*, 'marvels of originality and thought', according to Campos, that would supply the philosophical commentary to the work of the poets. In reality these works were never written. Pessoa wanted someone like Mora because he had a keen philosophical insight, but he did not have the kind of intellectual temperament that it takes to put together a philosophical discourse. And so, although Mora left behind many notes and comments, there was no work to bring him fully to life and he remained only a project of a heteronym.

Pessoa planned to develop the dramatics of his theatre further. He prepared accounts of how they first met and of some of the conversations that they were meant to have had. What exactly Pessoa hoped to create is not entirely clear, but whatever his projects were, they did not go very far. Judging from *The Mariner* and *The Anarchist Banker* a dramatic talent, most of all an ear for dialogue, was not Pessoa's forte. The few exchanges, mostly between Caeiro and Campos, are rather leaden, repetitive and do not add a great deal.

The interactions between the poets, although sketchy, do bring out one fundamental issue: Campos, Reis and Pessoa, all alike, considered Caeiro the Master. He founded the new paganism, and his insistence on the primacy of sensations acted like a cleansing ideology. It was he, not Pessoa himself, who was the first. In other words, Caeiro, the imaginary poet, influenced other imaginary poets and transformed his own creator to boot. The 'author' is displaced. He becomes several, responding to the teachings of the Master. The Master is not a person, he is a sage who embodies an idea, as Campos put it: 'he is not a pagan, he is paganism'. The beginning is innocence, before Christianity, before metaphysics, before man lost the paradise of pure existence. This is what Caeiro affirms. In fact, in the Pessoan constellation he is the one who is the most affirmative.

Campos is also affirmative, but only at the beginning. And, interestingly, Caeiro is also the only one who does not feel split into several personalities, quite the opposite, in the ninth poem of *The Keeper of Flocks* he declares, 'I feel my whole body lying on reality'. Caeiro affirms because he can still discover himself in what he sees, he is the innocent who has not experienced the schism that separates him from his sensations. He knows the state of real peace.

Pessoa was not always consistent in his attitude to the heteronyms. At times, probably when he was most immersed in the game, he thought of dramatising the heteronyms to the extreme, to the point where he would efface his own presence. In one account, not published by Pessoa but nevertheless polished as though in preparation for publication, we learn that Pessoa 'who does not exist, properly speaking' actually met Caeiro on that very 8th March 1914. It was on that occasion that he read *The Keeper of Flocks* and then ran home in a fever and wrote *Oblique Rain*. But there were also times when Pessoa seemed to lose his nerve. He would then feel personally responsible for the writings of the other poets. In one of the many 'introductions' to his heteronymic poetry he wrote:

> For some temperamental reason, which I do not propose to analyse, and which would not be important to analyse, I have constructed inside me various personae distinct from each other and from myself, personae to whom I have attributed various poems which are not like me, nor my sentiments and ideas, but which I have written.
>
> Such are the poems of Caeiro, of Ricardo Reis and of Álvaro de Campos. There is no point in searching for ideas and sentiments that are mine since many of them express ideas, which I don't accept and sentiments which I have never experienced. They should be simply read as they are, which is how one should read anyway.
>
> One example: I wrote the eighth poem of *The Keeper*

of Flocks with repugnance and I was startled with its infantile blasphemy and absolute antispiritualism. Myself, apparently real and living an objective social life, I don't use blasphemy nor am I antispiritualist.

Why Pessoa should write this we do not know, nor do we know when he wrote it, as the text is undated. One could venture a guess that it comes from a time when Pessoa was most removed from his heteronyms, possibly during one of his Sebastianist periods when indeed such anti-spiritualism would be unthinkable. Re-reading the poem upon coming across this declaration one finds it difficult to believe that repugnance was indeed Pessoa's 'real' feeling, however good he was at feigning. It is rather that this comment gives some indication as to why he prevaricated with publication.

When Pessoa was publishing the heteronyms in the early days he just let them out under their own names. It is quite possible that there were people who believed that these poets were real. In the end Pessoa decided to own up, so to speak. Still, he wanted the heteronyms to retain their independence. Thus he states in the letter, 'It is I who fabricated their ages and their lives', but then says that Campos' precise date of birth is confirmed by someone else and by a horoscope. The heteronyms were independent but their work was finally Pessoa's responsibility; this is how he wished it to be. Towards the end of his life Pessoa wrote a letter to Gaspar Simões concerning the possible book publication. He did give some thought as to how they should come out and no longer wanted them to appear just under their presumed names; it would no longer serve any purpose. He suggested that it would be best if they were presented as poems of Fernando Pessoa under an apt title *Fictions of the Interlude*. When Gaspar Simões and Luís de Montalvor prepared the first posthumous edition they followed this suggestion and that is how the poems became known.

The ingenuity of the way Pessoa addressed the question of

authorship has been much admired. In this post-modern age we like those who contribute to the death of the old ego. We admire Pessoa because he acted out the 'death of the Author', decades before the idea was articulated. How he experienced all this himself we can only speculate. It seems quite certain that this many-faceted inner life and obliteration of the central 'I' were not always easy to live with. So when we, the readers, explore Pessoa's theatre, amused and intrigued, we would do well to bear in mind an observation that he makes in *The Book of Disquiet*: 'we must remember that tragedies, for the aesthete, are interesting to observe but disconcerting to experience.' Whether he was referring to this break-up into several personalities is not at all certain, but these words do make one think.

III

In writing I rock myself,
like a crazed mother her dead child.
The Book of Disquiet

Pessoa, the inventor of fictional poets, was becoming known in Europe through a growing number of translations and his heteronymic strategy was attracting increasingly more critical attention. Nothing like it had ever been seen before and it ensured Pessoa's reputation as one of the great Modernists. Then in 1982, almost half a century after his death, another publication appeared—*The Book of Disquiet.*This was a sensation. To many it is the poet's real masterpiece and it is Pessoa's most read book.

Attentive readers would have spotted a few fragments that Pessoa had published during his life, and a few more that had appeared since, but only those who had access to the manuscripts had any idea of the scale of the work. What no one knows is what it would have looked like had Pessoa completed it. He began writing it in 1913, that is before the heteronyms were born, and continued working on it, on and off, until his death. Already in 1914 he mentions it in a letter, 'it's all fragments, fragments, fragments'. And so it remained—a hopelessly unfinished book of fragments. Shortly before his death Pessoa marked an envelope L. do. D. (*Livro do Desassossego*, The Book of Disquiet) and shoved into it various fragments of prose which he had been composing all his literary life. Those were the preparatory stages to hone the work into a publishable form and that was all that Pessoa had time to do; he never got around to appointing a literary executor, nor did he leave any precise indications as to how he would arrange the material. Some of the fragments were finished and polished; many others were still in manuscript, sometimes barely legible, sometimes no more than loose notes. To aggravate the situation further,

Pessoa's own selection turned out to be unreliable. Some fragments found in the envelope did not seem to belong in *The Book of Disquiet* and among the rest of his papers others were found that obviously did. All this renders a definitive edition impossible, though obviously it must at the same time remain an aim. Who knows, maybe Pessoa, ever amused by variability, would like it this way.

There were two major periods of activity when the book was written, the first between 1913 and 1917, and the second between 1929 and 1934. The twenties are thought to be Pessoa's fallow years, although this is not all that certain, as only a few fragments from before 1929 are dated. The same year in which he started writing the book, in 1913, Pessoa published a fragment from it, 'In the Forest of Estrangement'. This symbolist, heavily aestheticised, dream-like poetic prose did not turn out to be characteristic of the rest of *Disquiet*, or at least there are not many similar fragments in the book. Over time it changed considerably. It became something like an existential diary, a place where Pessoa, the spectator watching the world pass by, would jot down observations, thoughts, meditate on the human condition, and, most of all, on himself. In parts it reminds one of Nietzsche in his aphoristic mode, in parts it reminds one of Rilke in *Malte Laurids Brigge*.

The project was never systematic and went in different directions. The authorship also changed. It began as a book written by Vicente Guedes, so like Pessoa himself that he provoked pity. At some point one Baron of Teive is mentioned in connection with it. But as the work progressed it began to acquire a distinct voice, that of an assistant bookkeeper, Bernardo Soares, who emerged, possibly as late as fifteen years after the writing had begun. After this voice had emerged Pessoa intended to revise the earlier fragments to conform to the 'true psychology' of Bernardo Soares. This is how the author of the book is described:

Nothing had ever obliged him to do anything. He had spent his childhood alone. He never joined any group. He never pursued a course of study. He never belonged to a crowd. The circumstances of his life were marked by that strange but rather common phenomenon—perhaps, in fact, it's true for all lives—of being tailored to the image and likeness of his instincts, which tended toward inertia and withdrawal.

He never had to face the demands of society or of the state. He even evaded the demands of his own instincts. Nothing ever prompted him to have friends or lovers.

(From the Preface)

Soares's life is reduced to the bare minimum. He lives alone in a rented room in Baixa, a commercial quarter in the centre of Lisbon. The quarter is lively and many of its streets are quite elegant, but rua dos Douradores, on which Soares lives and works, is an untypically dreary street. Soares rarely ventures out of his immediate neighbourhood. He works in a textile trading office down the road. His boss and two or three other employees in the same office are all the social contacts that he has. When not at work he roams the streets of Baixa or holes out in his room and writes his disquiet.

Many of Soares's traits resemble Pessoa himself. Loneliness, immobility, a meaningless office job were all part of Pessoa's existence. For that reason Pessoa did not consider Soares a fully independent heteronym but only a semi-heteronym and Pessoa referred to him as his mutilated self. By this he seemed to mean that Soares represented his impoverished self. The traits are the same but everything is shrunk. Pessoa was lonely but Soares's solitude is more extreme; Pessoa hardly travelled, but unlike Soares, who did not even seem to get as far as the harbour, Pessoa knew all of Lisbon intimately; and Pessoa also worked for a commerce firm, but his job was not a daily office grind. Stripping Soares of external accidents, through an aesthetics of poverty, abnegation, decadence and insignificance, Pessoa bares himself open. Soares's voice is sometimes what one imagines

Pessoa would sound like in a confessional mood. This is the nearest we get to Pessoa's pain, to Pessoa at his most intimate. Soares is the voice of Pessoa's poetic destiny and he writes it in prose.

> I consider poetry to be an intermediate stage between music and prose. Like music, poetry is bound by rhythmic laws, and even when these are not the strict laws of metre, they still exist as checks, constraints, automatic mechanisms of repression and censure. In prose we speak freely. We can incorporate musical rhythms, and still think. We can incorporate poetic rhythms, and yet remain outside them. An occasional poetic rhythm won't disturb prose, but an occasional prose rhythm makes poetry fall down. (227)

Pessoa also made another important observation: it is easier to feign in verse than in prose. This is perhaps because rhyme, rhythm, the poetic syntax not only limit but also lead away, away from the 'I' that writes. Prose tends towards precision; it attempts to render the impression or feeling as closely as possible. But maybe Pessoa had something else in mind.

> I see life as a roadside inn where I have to stay until the coach from the abyss pulls up. I don't know where it will take me, because I don't know anything. I could see this inn as a prison, for I'm compelled to wait in it; I could see it as a social centre, for it's here that I meet others. But I'm neither impatient nor common. I leave who will to stay shut up in their rooms, sprawled out on beds where they sleeplessly wait, and I leave who will to chat in the parlours, from where their songs and voices conveniently drift out here to me. I'm sitting at the door, feasting my eyes and ears on the colours and sounds of the landscape, and I softly sing—for myself alone—wispy songs I compose while waiting.
> Night will fall on us all and the coach will pull up. I enjoy the breeze I'm given and the soul I was given to enjoy it with, and I no longer question or seek. If what I write in the book of travellers can, when read by others

at some future date, also entertain them on their journey, then fine. If they don't read it, or are not entertained, that's fine too. (1)

So all that Soares possesses is senses, the eyes and ears to feast on colours and sounds, the soul to enjoy the breeze. This is what Caeiro taught. And like all the others Soares admires Caeiro and he even quotes these lines from the seventh poem of *The Keeper of Flocks*: 'Because I'm the size of what I see / And not the size of my stature'.

But nothing of Caeiro's simplicity follows. Soares rarely experiences the breeze, and the colours and sounds of landscape are those of the city. Instead of sitting at the door, he looks from a window high up. The rooftops, the sky, the sounds coming from the street below—these are his usual sensations. But nothing touches him more than the sky. Its endless perturbations and the rain fill Soares with foreboding.

> Something still more portentous, like a black expectation, now hovered in the air, so that even the rain seemed intimidated; a speechless darkness fell over the atmosphere. And suddenly, like a scream, a dreadful day shattered. The light of a cold hell swept through the contents of all things, filling minds and crannies. Everything gaped in awe, and then heaved a sigh of relief, for the strike had passed. The almost human sound of the sad rain was happy. Hearts automatically pounded hard, and thinking made one dizzy. A vague religion formed in the office. No one was himself, and Senhor Vasques appeared at the door of his office to say he didn't quite know what. Moreira smiled, the fringes of his face still yellow from the sudden fright, and his smile was no doubt saying that the next bolt of thunder would strike further away. A swift wagon loudly broke in on the usual noises from the street. The telephone shivered uncontrollably. Instead of retreating to his private office, Vasques stepped toward the phone in the common office. There was a respite, a silence, and the rain fell like a nightmare. Vasques forgot about the phone, which had stopped ringing. The office

boy fidgeted in the back of the office like a bothersome object.

An enormous joy, full of deliverance and peace of mind, disconcerted us all. We returned to our work a bit light-headed, becoming spontaneously sociable and pleasant with each other. Without being told to, the office boy opened wide the windows. The fragrance of something fresh entered with the damp air into the office. The now gentle rain fell humbly. The sounds from the street, which were the same as before, were different. We could hear the voices of the wagoners, and they were really people. The clear-ringing bells of the trams a block over participated in our sociability. A lone child's burst of laughter was like a canary in the limpid atmosphere. The gentle rain tapered off.

It was six o'clock. The office was closing. Through the half-open door of his private office Senhor Vasques said, 'You can all go now,' pronouncing the words like a business benediction. I immediately stood up, closed the ledger and put it away. I returned my pen with a deliberate gesture to its place in the inkstand, walked toward Moreira while pronouncing a 'See you tomorrow' full of hope, and then shook his hand as if he'd done me a big favour. (450)

In this beautiful fragment, as in the rest of the book, we find something best called a meteorology of sensations, which is also a meteorology of fear, of promise and of dejection. No one has seen the sky like Soares, and it is far removed from Caeiro's unperturbed calm. 'Since the dull beginning of the hot, deceitful day, dark clouds with jagged edges had been ranging over the oppressed city. Towards the estuary they were grimly piled one on top the other, and as they spread, so did a forewarning of tragedy . . . a dire expectation hung in the pallid atmosphere.' (183) 'There's something of my disquiet in the endless drizzle, then shower, then drizzle, then shower, through which the day's sorrow uselessly pours itself out over the earth.' (141) Caeiro was the Argonaut of the senses, Pessoa of the feigned sensations; Soares is an Argonaut of pathological sensibility (124). But he is lucid. With a precision of an existential surgeon he dissects his feelings, studies his anxieties, lays open his pain. He suffers from self-consciousness. Holding in front of himself a merciless mirror, without hope or nostalgia, he is afflicted by the disease that comes from being able to see oneself. The end of this journey is tedium, 'Yes, tedium is the loss of the soul's capacity for self-delusion; it is the mind's lack of the non-existent ladder by which it might firmly ascend to truth' (263).

Soares destroys himself. He has no inner self and thus he has to conjure up a space where he can create various other personalities. He is multiple, 'the self who disdains his surroundings is not the same as the self who suffers or takes joy in them. In the vast colony of our being there are many species of people who think and feel in different ways' (396). This multiplicity is a familiar theme of all of Pessoa's thought; the self is a stage on which a multi-character drama is acted out. The true self is a multiple self, a self that changes, splinters, a self that is everywhere and nowhere. But something goes wrong. The incessant probing and delving reveals the soul as 'a madhouse of the grotesque. If a soul were able to reveal itself truthfully, if its shame and modesty didn't run deeper than all its known and named ignominies, then it would be—as is said of truth—a well, but a sinister well full of murky echoes and inhabited by abhorrent creatures, slimy non-beings, lifeless slugs, the snot of subjectivity' (242). Yes, Soares is very lucid. He does not spare himself. Truth is a horror.

Soares travels, not for real, naturally, but in his imagination. Real travel nauseates him; tedium is absent only from landscapes that don't exist (122). Like Campos he also once takes to the sea, 'It was on a vaguely autumnal twilight hour that I set out on the journey I never made' ('A Voyage I Never Made (I)', p.460). He visits faraway places but the voyage is feeble, his imagination does not draw in. For one, he does not even go to a real harbour to watch real steamers, as Campos did in 'Maritime Ode', to set off on his imaginary trip. Besides, Soares is too lucid to lose himself in the kind of exuberance that drove Campos on his voyages.

And much as he tries to convince himself that the imaginary can take him elsewhere, to the space of non-I, much as he tries to convince himself that he is multiple, he is dragged back by a dull pain. Ever present, it never seems to leave him. The pain is such that Soares is at times full of self-pity. He is lonely; he is a nobody. He believes in solitude and renunciation, 'the best and most regal course is to abdicate' (105). He rejects external reality, he does not wish for anything. He is forgotten by others 'And when I leaned out from my high window, looking down at the street I couldn't see, I suddenly felt like one of those damp rags used for house cleaning that are taken to the window to dry but are forgotten, balled up, on the sill where they slowly leave a stain' (29). Soares often describes his state in a curious double negative. He looks down on a street that he cannot see, he interrupts what he is not thinking, or repudiates what he does not feel. Systematically stripping away all that others cling to, Soares arrives at a self-definition—he is a vacant interlude between two negatives. 'I'm the bridge between what I don't have and what I don't want.' (232), his consciousness is a 'confused series of intervals between non-existent things' (442). An absolute emptiness, a desert on which nothing grows, envelopes him. 'No feeling in the world can lift my head from the pillow where I've let it sink in desperation, unable to deal with my body or with the idea that I'm alive, or even with the abstract idea of life'. ('Apocalyptic Feeling', p. 398)

All that Soares can do is write. Perhaps he should not. After all, what can writing bring to someone so tormented? He himself wonders about this: 'why do I keep writing? Because I still haven't learned to practise completely the renunciation that I preach. I haven't been able to give up my inclination to poetry and prose. I have to write as if I were fulfilling a punishment' (231). He writes to cure his desolation (144). And also: 'For me, to write is self-deprecating, and yet I can't quit doing it. Writing is like the drug I abhor and keep taking, the addiction I despise and depend on' (152). Soares cannot not write. He hopes to pour out of himself into the depth of paper all his anxiety; writing is his fight for survival. And he discovers the impossibility of this task. It is worse than an impossibility. As the writing progresses it becomes more incisive and with it the pain more acute. It spills out everywhere, its meanings multiply but it will not go away. Words enclose Soares, condemning him to who he is. And so, at one point he declares: 'I chose the wrong method of escape' (462), and in the same fragment, 'I killed my will by analysing it. If only I could return to my childhood before analysis, even if it would have to be before I had a will!'.

The Book of Disquiet gives the strongest glimpse into Pessoa's sense of lost childhood. His father died when he was five, Soares did not lose his father when a child, but his mother. This displacement may in fact be closer to Pessoa's own feelings. He never seems to have referred to the death of his father but by all accounts he suffered after his mother re-married and he also suffered later when he was separated from her. When she died Pessoa was devastated. But rarely has he been as poignant as here through Soares:

> I'm so cold, so weary in my abandonment. Go and find my Mother, O Wind. Take me in the Night to the house I never knew. Give me back my nursemaid, O vast Silence, and my crib and the lullaby that used to put me to sleep. (88)

And then, at times, comes a whiff of that lost past, the memory of the taste of chocolate (400), for example, so tangible and real that it seems a real memory of the 'real' Pessoa, going back to the mythical time before his father's disappearance and his mother's second marriage.

In some respects The Book of Disquiet reads like a companion to the heteronyms. All the themes are present: Caeiro's sensationism, Campos's imaginary travel, Reis's polytheism. In fact, we also find more or less everything else that we find in the poetry of Pessoa, everything else except Sebastianism—of this, not a word. The themes are there but with a difference. The heteronyms have their verses, they can act out their dreams, create new worlds. Soares cannot and does not. The prose has become his mirror, and 'the inventor of the mirror poisoned the human heart' (466). 'This book is a lament. Once written, it will replace *Alone* [by António Nobre] as the saddest book in Portugal' (412).

If *The Book of Disquiet* were no more than this lament, if it were no more than the anguish of self-discovery, of the discovery of the non-self that does not exist but feels and in its most truthful moments is only capable of experiencing solitude and pain, than the book would quickly become burdensome and tedious. It would certainly appeal to those who also experience pain and who seek camaraderie in suffering, elevating it to the status of sublimity, profundity and even ultimate truth. Pessoa would probably detest that. He observed wryly: 'Sometimes I think I must enjoy suffering. But I know I'd really prefer something else' (429). *Disquiet* is not just an artistically refined dirge, a complaint made musical and pleasing. There is much more than that. Part of the book's power lies in Pessoa's remarkable intelligence. He uses it to dissect his own condition but he also uses it to write maxims, develop an aesthetics, make psychological observations and comment on the spiritual sickness of his age. Placed on the margins he observes the disintegration of the Christian value system. People are no longer capable of believing, nor are they capable of disbelieving. This is the time of decadence. Each is locked away in his own solitude and 'we're all used to thinking of ourselves as primarily mental realities, and of other people as immediately physical realities' (338).

Soares is also a philosopher. In an aphoristic form, which suits his temperament best, he makes remarks that are quick to the point. He is not a philosopher in the strict sense, busying himself solving some problems; it is more the stance from which he looks. Like Caeiro, or Reis, he does not like metaphysics; it strikes him as a 'prolonged form of latent insanity' (87). Mostly he adopts a stoic position. Often he simply amuses himself, constructing little hypotheses, which he does not necessarily believe in—they are just games. But his most penetrating insights deal with the nature of reality and language. He is impatient with those who spend all their energy studying the language of Gods without leaving any for the colour and syntax of the language of men (256), a comment that applies, incidentally, to many of Pessoa's own writings on occult and related subjects. Soares really understands language. He knows it can shape ideologies and religions and the one remark that encapsulates his views best states that 'there is no enduring emotion without syntax. Immortality depends on the grammarians' (228).

The Book of Disquiet is one of the most moving literary testimonies of a tortured twentieth-century soul. Aloof from everything, untouched by ambition, aspiration, pretence, Soares discovers that, like everyone else, he is an insignificant human being lost in a huge modern crowd. The crowd cannot agree on anything so there is no point in trying to agree with it. But still, the streets are real and are filled with real people, milling around, selling newspapers, working in offices and barbershops. The streets of Lisbon are alive. The same shouts, the familiar tingling of trams, the heat, the rain, the place of birth where Pessoa discovers that his nation is the Portuguese language and the beautiful Lisbon his home. He is no different than other of his city's inhabitants. Just like them he came along and just like them he will pass. His presence will be noted by only a few and he will be quickly forgotten, just like everyone else. Only that his writing, 'the silent shout that there's a soul there' (25), left behind a mark deeper than he could have ever himself imagined.

IV

One day, when everything is finally and fully revealed, that other door will open and all that we were—rubbish of stars and souls—will be swept outside the house, so that what exists can begin again.

The Book of Disquiet

The Book of Disquiet is the last major stroke in the Pessoa portrait. More fine poems have been since found, more may perhaps still surface, but it is hard to imagine that the famous trunk still holds unknown works important enough to significantly shift perceptions. The picture is complex and full of contradictions. Pessoa cultivated in his lifetime the image of a Sebastianist poet and fostered a posthumous reputation of a Modernist; he was a nationalist, anglophile and cosmopolitan, a great poet who could write badly, an author of political pamphlets and of one of this century's great confessional writings. He was drawn to mysticism, the occult, secret religious societies, futurism and modernity. He wrote poems in French and English, as well as in his native Portuguese; he regularly contributed to a crossword competition in England; he drew astrological horoscopes of everyone, of his heteronyms, of King Sebastian and of Portugal itself; he dabbled in numerology and in kabbala. Pessoa means 'person' in Portuguese but it also derives from 'persona', the mask. Like a trickster Pessoa would pull out one mask after another. He changed them incessantly. Some he put on many times, some only once. Some of them stuck, others were discarded. The audience, ever enchanted, has been left watching the spectacle, trying to fathom who Pessoa really was. Some think Campos is closest to the real Pessoa, some Soares; perhaps as a Sebastianist Pessoa was at his truest. While many have been guessing, the 'real' Pessoa 'who does not exist, properly speaking' has been effacing his presence leaving behind masks. There is an Oriental proverb that says that the number of masks it takes to picture an empty face is infinite.

The spectacle has lasted for a long time. During his life Pessoa revealed only a little. This was enough to gain him recognition and some admiration from his contemporaries. His status today is due to the immense number of posthumous publications. No other poet exists as much through the work of others as Pessoa does. He is a creation of those who arrange his manuscripts, prepare definitive versions of his works and publish unknown material, of those who write critical studies, and of the translators. They decipher the masks and they create the vast readership. To read Pessoa is to enter the labour of others. The timid Pessoa has drawn many people into his world.

It took some time before the Portuguese began any systematic arrangement of Pessoa's writings. The first great editorial undertaking came from João Gaspar Simões and Luís de Montalvor, who arranged the first editions in book form of the heteronymic poetry and of Pessoa himself (1942, Pessoa; 1944, Campos; 1946, Caeiro and Reis). In 1946, Jorge de Sena, another of Portugal's outstanding literary figures, prepared a collection of Pessoa's theoretical writings. Two more important volumes appeared some twenty years later under the editorship of the Austrian scholar Georg Rudolf Lind and Jacinto do Prado Coelho. These include some letters, Pessoa's writings on aesthetics, literary criticism, meditations on the relation between genius, art and madness, the endless attempts at preparing introductions for his work and of the *Orpheu* group. They also include many fragments of Pessoa's self-analysis. Two volumes, in which Pessoa's various notes on philosophy are collected have been edited by António de Pina Coelho. They come mostly from his youth and have little intrinsic (philosophical) interest, except that they show how seriously Pessoa studied the subject. In Brazil there is a single volume edition of all Pessoa's poetry edited by Maria Aliete Galhoz, who also supplied an excellent introduction. This could have been the best handy single edition available; it is however not reliable, as a number of readings of the manuscripts are inaccurate, and many important poems that have been found since the volume's first edition in 1960 are not included. Another volume, edited by Cleonice Berardinelli, contains the works in prose. The organization of the texts is not very clear, it could be better annotated, and it is not easy to find one's way around it; it also suffers from reading problems similar to the poetry volume. These were all one-off publications; the first comprehensive undertaking was the eleven-volume edition from the Lisbon publisher Ática that appeared between 1976 and 1981.

Pessoa scholarship has always posed serious difficulties. To begin with, the trunk with the manuscripts belonged to the family; access to it was haphazard, and some papers have probably disappeared. In 1966 his writings were bought by the National Library and catalogued, and a larger number of researchers gained access to the papers. It quickly transpired that due to the dishevelled state of these papers—some in handwriting that is difficult to decipher, some finished but with numerous variants on the margins that Pessoa still planned to consider—the available editions were not complete and some had dubious readings. In 1988 an official working group was set up to prepare a definitive critical edition. We get some idea of the difficulties that this enterprise entails from the fact that it was not an acknowledged Pessoa scholar who was appointed to head the group but a specialist in medieval manuscripts, Ivo de Castro. It was he who subjected the 1914 manuscripts to a detailed analysis and exploded the myth of the 8th of March one-off poetic revelation. The myth had been alive for a long time and de Castro's findings came to some as a considerable shock.

However, progress on the critical edition has been slow and in the meantime, in 1999, the Lisbon publisher Assírio & Alvim started a 24 volume edition, which will bring together practically all of Pessoa's writings. This edition will no doubt render the previous ones more or less obsolete. However, the editors have followed the already established practice of modernising Pessoa's spelling. He did not accept the new rules that were introduced in his time and in some works, particularly poems of Ricardo Reis and *Message*, he is quite archaic; some readers might want to consult older versions that reproduce the original spelling. (So, for example, Jonathan Griffin's translation of *Mensagem*, which is the only bilingual version, follows the original spelling from the Ática edition.) In the last two years Assírio & Alvim have also brought out a seven volume *Obra Essencial*, under the editorship of the Lisbon-based American scholar Richard Zenith. This shortened edition should satisfy the needs of most of Pessoa enthusiasts.

Of all of the works *The Book of Disquiet* has given most difficulties. The first edition took years to prepare. To begin with, it was coordinated by Jorge de Sena, but since he was living in America it proved technically impossible, and the final version was prepared under the editorship of Jacinto do Prado Coelho, Maria Aliete Galhoz and Teresa Sobral Cunha. Since then many other fragments belonging to the book have been found, and clearly a new edition was called for; it was prepared by Sobral Cunha. It has the first volume authored both by Bernardo Soares and his predecessor Vicente Guedes. Not many agreed with this decision. The latest version of *Disquiet*, prepared by Richard Zenith, appeared in the Assírio and Alvim *Obras de Fernando Pessoa* (volume V). Zenith kept the early symbolist, usually titled, texts in a separate section at the end, and arranged all the other fragments, as of a single author, attempting to give them some rhythm as they unfold. He also supplies a concordance table referring the reader to the manuscript, which can be consulted in the National Library in Lisbon. Such a scholarly apparatus may matter to only a few but, considering the state of the original—it is no more than a heap of fragments, some finished and typed, some just scribbled down—it is quite amazing that Zenith was the first to think of supplying this concordance table. This version is likely to remain the standard one for a long time, as it has already appeared in some dozen translations, including French,

German and English, and apparently Ivo de Castro's group are not planning to include *Disquiet* in their critical edition.

Apart from the efforts to bring Pessoa's unpublished work to light there has been a growing body of critical writings. It began with Gaspar Simões and Casais Monteiro who wrote the first book length biography and critical study, respectively. Of the other authors the most influential have been Eduardo Lourenço, Teresa Rita Lopes and José Gil. In his numerous writings Lourenço explored particularly well the wider cultural frame in which Pessoa worked; Teresa Rita Lopes is a great specialist in Portuguese Modernism as well as Pessoa and has done most to penetrate Pessoa's heteronymic work—she tracked down the seventy-two names, potential heteronyms that appear in Pessoa's papers; José Gil, a philosopher whose leanings place him close to some contemporary French thinkers, particularly Gilles Deleuze, carried out a perceptive analysis of the place of sensations in Pessoa's universe.

In other countries the appreciation of Pessoa came a little, but not much, later. In France it has been particularly strong. The groundwork was laid down by Pessoa's first translator, Pierre Hourcade. In 1960 there was already a book-length appraisal by Armand Guibert. To the French he is now a household name. The same is the case in Italy, Spain and Germany, largely due to the work of some outstanding figures who introduced Pessoa in their countries—Antonio Tabucchi in Italy, Ángel Crespo in Spain, Georg Rudolf Lind to the German speaking readership. He has also been translated into virtually all other European languages, as well as Chinese, Japanese and a few more.

Pessoa has been translated extensively into English as well. In 1971 two selections of poetry were published, one by Peter Rickard, the other by F.E.G. Quintanilha. Both are bilingual, and both have helpful introductions and notes. In the seventies there was a series of translations by J.C.R. Green. These have been followed by translations by Jonathan Griffin, Edwin Honig (usually in tandem with Susan M. Brown), and Keith Bosley. Most of these are out of print. The most recent work comes from the hands of Chris Daniels and Richard Zenith. With a few exceptions all the poetry translations used in this text have been chosen primarily for reasons of availability and do not necessarily reflect personal preference; all of them, at any rate, are fine.

The Book of Disquiet has had four translators, Margaret Jull Costa, Alfred Mac Adam, Iain Watson and Richard Zenith. (Zenith has worked on the text twice. His Assírio & Alvim version, published in English by Penguin, follows, and has rendered obsolete, the earlier Carcanet edition.) Since the other three translations are selections, the choice is obvious. In other countries heavily edited versions have also appeared. This is perhaps understandable. Because of the state of the manuscript, the temptation to make cuts is obvious. But whichever way this is done the work is poorer for it. It is like leaving out the repetitions from a Bach score. As a result the work is tighter but something goes missing. The wide acceptance of Zenith's recent edition will probably bring the truncated versions to an end.

This brings us to a curious situation concerning the reception of Pessoa in the English speaking countries. He has been extensively translated, many of his poems several times. Despite all this he remains little known and his name has not attained the kind of familiarity that the names of Cavafy, Mandelstam or Lorca have. Why this should be is hard to tell. Perhaps there still needs to be a major in-depth presentation of this fascinating figure.

Within a few decades of his death Pessoa grew from a great poet to a national monument, from a great Portuguese poet to a key figure of European Modernism, and Lisbon became a place of pilgrimage for those who fell under his spell. His remains have been moved from his burial place to the Jerónimos Monastery and now they share an abode with Luís de Camões. A bronze statue adorns an outside table of a café, which he frequented. No other modern poet occupies such a prominent place in a people's culture as Pessoa in Portugal. Pessoa has entered the collective psyche, if such a thing exists, of the Portuguese people. He is not a new incarnation of Sebastian, nor a supra-Camões but a phenomenon all of its own. His life continues far beyond the many literary commentaries that have been written since his death. Beginning with Almada Negreiros, Pessoa's old companion from the *Orpheu* days who had a long and creative life, almost every major Portuguese artist has painted a posthumous portrait of Pessoa and he has become part of the country's iconography. And he is also inseparable from his heteronymic companions Alberto Caeiro, Álvaro de Campos, Ricardo Reis, Bernardo Soares; we know their names, we know what they were like and we refer to them, naturally, without thinking, as to real beings, their poetry is their living tissue. They have their readers and commentators. So in a way their lives went on as well, more than their creator ever thought they would, none more so than in the case of Ricardo Reis. As we remember, he had been living in Brazil where he went into voluntary exile; as a monarchist he did not want to remain in the new republic. He would have probably lived out his days there, working as a doctor, had it not been for a telegram that he received from Campos telling him of the death of Pessoa. Campos was leaving for Scotland; Reis decided, there and then, to return to Lisbon, perhaps for good. Thus begins the novel *The Year of the Death of Ricardo Reis* by José Saramago, the great contemporary Portuguese writer. Reis returns to the Lisbon that Pessoa has just left. He takes up comfortable residence in a hotel and begins to reacquaint himself with his native land; he has sixteen years to catch up with. He meets Pessoa who, after his death, is given nine months to appear to those who matter to him. This is life's symmetry—nine months from conception to birth, the same from death to oblivion. They do not meet frequently, but when they do they talk about poetry, occasionally about politics and about what is happening in Reis's life. Shortly after moving into the hotel he begins a sexual liaison with a chambermaid. He also falls in love with another woman who is staying with her father in the same hotel. She is from the upper middle class; she is repressed and has a paralysed arm. No question of sex here. Reis's aimless but peaceful existence is interrupted by Salazar's secret police. They invite him for a little chat to their headquarters. Any charges against him? No, just checking up on this new arrival from exile, perhaps he is up to something. The police are not convinced that he is indeed the anti-socialist and anti-communist who never engages in any political activity; he did after all once quit the country for political reasons, and perhaps he is not as innocent as he appears. Nothing happens but the police decide to make enquiries into Reis's movements. The hotel manager quickly hears of this through his network of informants and the atmosphere becomes unpleasant. Reis rents an apartment and moves out. His new place is overlooking the statue of the sea monster Adamastor. He also finds a locum position in a practice in the centre of Lisbon on the Praça de Camões, from which he can see the Bard standing on the pedestal. The chambermaid becomes his charwoman and their relationship continues. Meetings with the other woman also continue. And around him, heartened by the developments in Germany and Italy and the progress of the civil war in Spain, the machine of the Salazar regime is in full swing. These are the bare essentials from which Saramago spins a magic web. Saramago brings Reis to life. But there is perhaps a polemical edge to the book because he brings Reis to an existence that is irrelevant and out of touch. He also makes Reis confront issues that Pessoa, for one reason or another, chose not to face fully—women, Camões, and the new political order into which his country was sinking. Of course, Saramago is playing with loaded dice. We realise this as soon as we try to imagine how different the book would be if it were about the last year of the unruly Álvaro de Campos. But polemical or not, this is a subtle homage and engagement coming from a writer from the next generation, a response of a kind which is probably unique in modern literature. It says something about Pessoa's posthumous power; it is a work by

Saramago, but it is also part of the Pessoa phenomenon. And it will last longer than any commentary because it is simply a beautiful and wise novel. It brings us close to the Lisbon that Pessoa knew. Saramago makes the streets tactile; we can smell them, see them and stroll along them together with Reis. And the rain, the very same rain that was so often present in Pessoa's poems, and which filled Bernardo Soares with foreboding, is there. Reis arrives from his Brazilian exile to a downpour. A thick black cloud is enveloping the city, everything is wet; the station by the harbour is flooded. As it happens, Saramago did not make this up, this is how it really was: after Pessoa's death the rain did not seem to stop for weeks on end.

The Tobacconist's

I am nothing.
I shall always be nothing.
I can only want to be nothing.
Apart from this, I have in me all the dreams in the world.

Windows of my room,
The room of one of the world's millions whom no-one knows
(And if they knew me, what would they know?),
You face the mystery of a street crossed constantly by people,
A street that is inaccessible to any thought,
Real, impossibly real, certain, unknowably certain,
With the mystery of things beneath the stones and the living,
With death putting dampness on walls and white hairs on men,
With Destiny driving the cart of everything down the road of
    nothing.

Today I am defeated, as if I knew the truth.
Today I am lucid, as if I were about to die
And had no greater brotherhood with things
Than a farewell, this house and this side of the street
Transformed into a row of railway carriages, and a departure
    whistled
Inside my head,
And a jolting of nerves and a grinding of bones in the going.

Today I am perplexed, like someone who has thought and found
    and forgotten.
Today I am divided between the loyalty I owe
To the Tobacconists's across the street, as a real external thing
And the feeling that all is a dream, as a real internal thing.

I have failed in everything.
But since I had no purpose, everything may have been nothing.
From the apprenticeship they gave me,
I climbed down through the window at the back of the house.
I went into the country full of purpose.

But all I found was grass and trees,
And when there were people, they were like the others.
I leave the window, and sit down on a chair. Of what shall I think?

What do I know of what I shall be, I who don't know what I am?
Be what I think? But I think of being so many things!
And there are so many who think of being the same thing that
    there cannot be so many!
Genius? At this very moment
A hundred thousand brains are dreaming they are geniuses like me,
And history will not record—who knows?—a single one,
And nothing will be left but dung of all those future conquests.
No, I don't believe in me . . .
In how many attics and non-attics in the world
Are there geniuses-to-themselves dreaming even now?
How many lofty and noble and lucid aspirations—
Yes, truly lofty and noble and lucid—
And even feasible, perhaps,
Will never see the light of day, nor find an ear to listen?
The world is for those born to conquer it
And not for those who dream they can, even if they could.
I have dreamed more than Napoleon accomplished.
I have clasped to my hypothetical breast more humanities than
    Christ,
I have made philosophies in secret that no Kant ever wrote.
But I am, and perhaps shall always be, the man in the attic,
Even though I don't live in the attic;
I shall always be 'the one who was not born for that';
I shall always be merely 'the one who had qualities';
I shall always be man who waited for someone to open the door
    near a wall without a door,
And sang the song of the Infinite in the chicken coop,
And heard the voice of God in a covered well.
Believe in me? No. In nothing.
Let nature pour upon my burning head
Her sun, her rain, the wind that finds my hair,
And let the rest come, if it does or must, or let it not come.
Heart-sick slaves of the stars,
We conquer the world before we get out of bed;

But we wake up and find it opaque,
We get up and find it alien,
We leave the house and the world is the whole earth,
Plus the solar system and the Milky Way and the Undefined.

(Eat your chocolates, little girl;
Eat chocolates!
Chocolates are really the only metaphysics in the world
And all religions teach you no more than the confectioner's.
Eat, messy little girl, eat!
If only I could eat chocolates with the same truth as you do!
But I think, and when I unwrap the silver paper, which is really only
    tin foil,
I throw it all onto the floor, as I have thrown away my life.)

But at least of the bitterness of what I'll never be there will remain
The rapid scribbling of these lines,
A broken casement opening on the Impossible.
But at least I can award myself a contempt without tears,
Noble at last in the open-handed way with which I throw
The dirty linen which is me, without a laundry list, into the course
    of things,
And stay at home without a shirt.

(You, who console, who don't exist and therefore console,
Whether a Greek goddess, conceived as living stone,
Or a patrician Roman matron, impossibly noble and wicked,
Or a princess of the troubadours, gentle and fair,
Or an eighteenth century marquise, aloof in a low-cut gown,
Or a famous cocotte of my father's generation,
Or else some modern counterpart—I cannot quite think what—
All of this, whatever you may be, be so, if it can inspire me, let it!

My heart is an empty bucket.
Like those who invoke spirits invoke spirits I invoke
Myself and find nothing.
I go to the window and see the street with absolute clarity.
I see shops, I see pavements, I see passing cars,
I see living creatures in clothes who pass each other by,

I see dogs who also exist,
And all of this weighs on me like being sent into exile,
And all of this is alien, like everything else.)

I have lived, studied, loved and even believed,
And today there isn't a beggar I don't envy for not being me.
I see each one's rags and his running sores and his lies,
And think: perhaps you never lived nor studied nor loved nor
    believed
(Because it's possible to do these things without really having done
    them);
Perhaps you simply existed, like a lizard whose tail's been severed
And the tail goes on wriggling on this side of the lizard.

I have made myself what I did not know,
And what I could have made myself I did not.
The domino I put on was the wrong one.
They knew me at once for someone else and I didn't deny this and
    was lost.
When I wanted to remove the mask,
It was stuck to my face.
When I took it off and saw myself in the mirror,
I had grown old.
I was drunk, and I could not wear the domino I hadn't taken off.
I threw away the mask and fell asleep in the cloakroom
Like a dog that's tolerated by the management
Because it's harmless
And I shall write this story to prove that I'm sublime.

Musical essence of my useless verses
If I could find you as something made by me
Instead of being stuck here, forever facing the Tobacconists's across
    the street,
Trampling on the awareness that I exist
Like a rug on which a drunkard trips
Or a doormat which the gypsies stole and was worth nothing.

But the Tobacconist has come to the door and is standing in his
    doorway.

I look at him with the discomfort of a half-turned head
And the discomfort of a half-understanding soul.
He will die and I shall die.
He will leave his signboard and I shall leave verses.
After a while the signboard will also die, and so will the verses
And after another while the street in which the signboard hung
        will die
And the language in which the verses were written.
And then the turning planet on which all of this took place.
On other satellites of other systems something like people
Will go on making things like verses and living under things like
        signboards,
Always one thing opposite the other,
Always one thing as useless as the other,
Always the impossible as stupid as the real,
Always the deepest mystery as certain as the sleep of mystery on
        the surface,
Always this or always something else or neither one thing nor the
        other.

But the man has gone into the Tobacconist's (to buy tobacco?)
And all at one plausible reality drops upon me.
I half-rise, energetic, full of conviction, human,
And decide to write these verses in which I say the opposite.
I light a cigarette at the thought of writing them
And savour in the cigarette release from any thought.
I follow the trail of smoke like a route of my own
And enjoy, for one sensitive and fitting moment,
Release from all speculations
And the awareness that metaphysics is a consequence of feeling
        out of sorts.

Then I sink into my chair
And carry on smoking.
As long as Destiny allows me, I'll go on smoking.
(If I married my washerwoman's daughter
Perhaps I would be happy).
This settled, I get up from the chair. I go to the window.

The man has come out of the Tobacconist's (slipping change into
    his trouser pocket?)
Ah, but I know him: it's Esteves sans metaphysics.
(The Tobacconist has come to the door).
As if by divine instinct Esteves has turned and seen me.
He waves a greeting, I shout 'Hello Esteves!', and the universe
Falls into place for me again without ideal or hope, and the
Tobacconist smiles.

Lisbon, 15th January, 1928
Translated by Suzette Macedo.

References and Notes

p.15 'It happens, that when looking . . .' Letter dated 24.6.1916. This
and all further quotes from letters can be found in *Obra Essencial
de Fernando Pessoa*, vol. 7, or in *Correspondência (1905–1922)*
and *Correspondência (1923–1935)*.

p.15 'I, of the race of Navigators . . .' in *Obra Essencial de Fernando
Pessoa*, vol. 3, p.286.

p.16 'I'd like to write the encomium . . .' fr. 322 in *The Book of
Disquiet*, tr. Richard Zenith, London and New York: Penguin,
2001.

p.18 'One can argue that the current political . . .' in *Obra Essencial*,
vol. 3, p.128.

p.18 'I have come to a full possession . . .' in *Obra Essencial*, vol. 5,
p.98.

p.21 'I have great admiration for Camões . . .' letter dated 11.12.
1931.

p.21 'There is only one period of creation . . .' *Obra Essencial*, vol. 3,
p. 200.

p.22 'This break-up into pseudonymic personalities . . .' letter dated
26.4.1919.

p.22 'And I am swaddled . . .' from 'Maritime Ode', in *Poems of
Fernando Pessoa*, tr. Edwin Honig and Susan M. Brown, New
York: The Ecco Press, 1986.

p.24 'I think it's not worth having gone . . .' tr. Honig and Brown
in *Poems of Fernando Pessoa*. The original title is 'Opiário', a
coinage, which in this instance has been translated as 'Opium
Eater' but perhaps would be better rendered as 'Opium Den'.
Keith Bosley solves the difficulty by making up an English
coinage and translates it as 'Opiary' in *A Centenary Pessoa*.

p.25 'Everything that I have written . . .' letter dated 19.1.1915.

p.28 'Rise in the sun in me . . .' in *Message*, tr. Jonathan Griffin,
London: The Menard Press/King's College London, 1992; 2nd
edn., Exeter: Shearsman Books/The Menard Press, 2007.

p.30 'Confused like the Universe . . .' in *Message*.

p.33 'Conservative in an English way . . .' Opening 'Autobiographical
Note' in *Obra Essencial*, vol. 5, p.134-5.

p.34 'Babylon's Lloyd Georges . . .' translated by Chris Daniels, *The
Collected Poems of Álvaro de Campos, Vol 1*, Exeter: Shearsman
Books, 2009.

p.35 'but I am also, mostly and often . . .' letter dated 13.1.1935.

p.40 'Some time around 1912 . . .' letter dated 13.1.1935.

p.41 'I desire to be a creator of myths . . .' in *Obra Essencial* vol. 5, p. 146.

p.43 'The scandal is enormous . . .' letter dated 4.4.1915.

p.44 'I don't believe in God . . .' from *The Keeper of Flocks*, collected in *The Collected Poems of Alberto Caeiro*, translated by Chris Daniels, Exeter: Shearsman Books, 2007. All further quotations from *The Keeper of Flocks* are from the same edition. The Roman numerals refer to the poem numbers as given by Pessoa.

p.45 'A poet of what may be called . . .' p.442, vol. II in *Pessoa por Conhecer* by Teresa Rita Lopes. Lisboa: Editorial Estampa, 1990.

p.46 'Sometimes I start looking at a stone' in *The Collected Poems of Alberto Caeiro, op.cit.*

p.50 'the only occult meaning of things . . .' trans. modified. Daniels (as well as other translators) has 'the only hidden meaning of things'. In the original Portuguese it is 'o único sentido oculto das coisas'. To translate this as 'the hidden meaning' would in every other circumstance be good, as it is poetically better and 'occult' is far more generic in Portuguese than in English. But since Caeiro is relating (possibly) to the occult I thought it better to retain the stricter 'occult'. As it happens, Pessoa himself also translated these very lines in one of his many English introductions to Caeiro and also keeps the 'occult.' (in *Pessoa por Conhecer*, vol II, p.439).

— 'But in the beginning was the Word . . .' in *Fernando Pessoa* tr. Jonathan Griffin, Penguin Books, Harmondsworth, 1982.

p.52 'Because feeling is like the sky . . .' tr. Griffin in *Fernando Pessoa*.

— 'They say I pretend or lie . . .' tr. Griffin in *Fernando Pessoa*.

p.53 'The poet is a feigner'. This poem has been translated into English about a dozen times and the opening line 'Um poeta e um fingidor', one of Pessoa's most famous lines, is always rendered differently—'The poet is good at pretending' (Rickard), 'The poet is an inventor' (Quintanilha), 'The poet is a faker' (Honig and Brown), 'The poet is a fake' (Bosley). The translation used here, which I like best, is by Jean Longland, first published in *Poet Lore*, New York, Autumn issue, 1970.

p.54 'but to one who hopes for nothing . . .' tr. Griffin in *Fernando Pessoa*.

— 'on their calm Olympus ...' in *Fernando Pessoa. Sixty Portuguese Poems*, tr. F.E.G. Quintanilha, Cardiff: University of Wales Press, 1971.

— 'I love the roses from the Garden of Adonis ...' tr. Chris Daniels and published online at his *Notes of a Weary Traveller* blog.

p.55 'Hate you, Christ, I do not ...' tr. Griffin in *Fernando Pessoa*.

p.56 'Legion live in us ...' tr. Griffin in *Fernando Pessoa*.

p.57 'In the painful light ...' tr. Chris Daniels in *The Collected Poems of Álvaro de Campos, Vol. 2*.

p.58 'I love and animate everything.' tr. Honig and Brown in *Poems of Fernando Pessoa*.

— 'Holding hands ...' from 'Salute to Walt Whitman', tr. Chris Daniels in *The Collected Poems of Álvaro de Campos, Vol. 1*.

— 'Go to hell without me ...' tr. Honig and Brown in *Poems of Fernando Pessoa*.

— 'Once again I see you ...' tr. Honig and Brown in *Poems of Fernando Pessoa*.

p.59 'I'm nothing ...' This poem, 'The Tobacco Shop' or 'The Tobacconists's', together with 'Autopsychography', is the most translated of Pessoa's poems. It has several fine renderings, including this one by Chris Daniels, from *The Collected Poems of Álvaro de Campos, Vol. 2*. A complete alternative version of the poem by Suzette Macedo, is offered as an appendix to this volume. It was first published in a bilingual edition by Calouste Gulbenkian Foundation, Lisbon, 1987.

p.59 'Not a minute too soon ...' tr. Richard Zenith in *Selected Poems of Fernando Pessoa & Co.*, New York: Harcourt Brace, 1966.

p.61 'A primrose by the river ...' *Obra Essencial*, vol. 3, p.81.

p.62 'I can *see* before me ...' letter dated 13.1.1935.

p.63 'an hour so deliciously mechanical ...' *Obra Essencial*, vol. 3, p. 275.

p.64 'He is not a pagan ...', *Obra Essencial*, vol. 3, p. 82.

p.65 'who does not exist ...', vol II, *Obra Essencial*, vol. 3, p. 97.

— 'For some temperamental reason ...', *Obra Essencial*, vol. 5, p. 151.

p.67 'we must remember that tragedies ...' *Book of Disquiet*, fr. 113.

p.73 'Nothing had ever obliged him ...' One should point out that, strictly speaking, this is probably Pessoa's description of the early author Vicente Guedes and not of Bernardo Soares. But this is the only description of the author of *Disquiet* that

Pessoa has left. But since it also suits Soares perfectly well, it is likely that Pessoa would have retained it had he completed the revision of the book.

p.74 'I consider poetry . . .' The numbers refer to the numbers of the fragments as in Zenith's translation in the Penguin 2001 edition.

Bibliography

Works by Fernando Pessoa

— *Obras Completas de Fernando Pessoa*. Lisbon: Ediçoes Ática, 11 volumes.
— *Obra Poética* in one volume, ed. Maria Aliete Galhoz, Rio de Janeiro: José Aguilar, 1960 (8th ed. 1981).
— *Obra em Prosa* in one volume, ed. Cleonice Berardinelli, Rio de Janeiro: Editora Nova Aguilar, 1974 (6th ed. 1990).
— *Livro do Desassossego por Bernardo Soares*, eds. Jacinto do Prado Coelho, Maria Aliete Galhoz and Teresa Sobral Cunha, Lisbon: Ática, 1982.
— *Livro do Desassossego*, vol I & II, ed. Teresa Sobral Cunha, Lisbon: Editorial Presença, 1990-1991.
— *Páginas de Doutrina Estética*, ed. Jorge de Sena, Lisbon: Inquérito, 1962.
— *Páginas Íntimas e de Auto-Interpretação*, ed. Georg Rudolf Lind and Jacinto do Prado Coelho, Lisbon: Ática, 1966.
— *Páginas de Estética e de Teoria e Crítica Literárias*, ed. Georg Rudolf Lind and Jacinto do Prado Coelho, Lisbon: Ática, 1966.
— *Textos Filosóficos*, ed. António de Pina Coelho. Lisbon: Ática, 1968, 2 vols.
— *Portugal, Sebastianismo e Quinto Imperio*, ed. António Quadros, Mem Martins: Publicaçoes Europa-America, 2005.
— *Pessoa por Conhecer*, vol II, ed. Teresa Rita Lopes, Lisbon: Editorial Estampa, 1990.
— *Obras de Fernando Pessoa*. 22 Volumes, Lisbon: Assírio & Alvim, 1998-2007
— Vol. 6: *Correspondência (1905–1922);*
— Vol. 7: *Correspondência (1923–1935);* both ed. Manuela Parrerira da Silva, 1999.
— *Obra Essencial de Fernando Pessoa*, 7 volumes, ed. Richard Zenith, Lisbon: Assírio & Alvim, 2006-2007

Translations into English

Poetry
— BOSLEY, Keith: in *A Centenary Pessoa*, Manchester: Carcanet, 1995. [89 poems].

— DANIELS, Chris: *The Collected Poems of Alberto Caeiro*, Exeter: Shearsman Books, 2007.

— DANIELS, Chris: *The Collected Poems of Álvaro de Campos*, vol. 1. Exeter: Shearsman Books, (forthcoming 2009).

— DANIELS, Chris: *The Collected Poems of Álvaro de Campos*, vol. 2. Exeter: Shearsman Books, 2008.

— GREEN, J.C.R.: *By Weight of Reason*, Shirley, Solihull, Warks: The Aquila Publishing Co. Ltd., 1968. [10 poems].

— GREEN, J.C.R.: *Álvaro de Campos. The Tobacconist*. Breakish, Isle of Skye: The Phaeton Press, The Aquila Publishing Co. Ltd., 1975. [12 poems].

— GREEN, J.C.R.: *Ricardo Reis. The Ancient Rhythm.* The Phaeton Press, Breakish, Isle of Skye: The Aquila Publishing Co. Ltd., 1976. [23 poems].

— GREEN, J.C.R.: *The Stations of the Cross.* Breakish, Isle of Skye: The Phaeton Press, The Aquila Publishing Co. Ltd. 1976. [25 poems].

— GREEN, J.C.R.: *The Keeper of Flocks.* Breakish, Isle of Skye: The Phaeton Press, The Aquila Publishing Co. Ltd., 1976. [19 poems].

— GREENE, James; MAFRA, Clara de Azevedo.: *Fernando Pessoa. The Surprise of Being.* London: Angel Books, 1986. [25 poems]. Bilingual.

— GRIFFIN, Jonathan: *Fernando Pessoa. Selected Poems.* London: Penguin Books, 1988. [106 poems].

— GRIFFIN, Jonathan: *Fernando Pessoa. Message.* London: The Menard Press/King's College, 1992. 2nd Edition, Exeter: Shearsman Books/Menard Press, 2007 [44 poems (complete)]. Bilingual.

— HONIG, Edwin; BROWN, Susan M.: *The Keeper of Sheep by Fernando Pessoa.* Riverdale-on-Hudson, NY: The Sheep Meadow Press, 1986 [49 poems (complete)].

— HONIG, Edwin; BROWN, Susan M.: *Poems of Fernando Pessoa.* New York: The Ecco Press, 1986. [129 poems + 22 English poems].

— LONGLAND, Jean R.: *Fernando Pessoa.* 'The Poet is a feigner' and other poems in *Poet Lore*, Autumn, 1970. [10 poems].

— MACEDO, Suzette: *The Tobacconist's. Tabacaria. A poem by Fernando Pessoa.* Lisbon: Calouste Gulbenkian Foundation, 1987. Bilingual.

— MERTON, Thomas: Twelve poems from *The Keeper of Sheep* in *Collected Poems of Thomas Merton*, New York: New Directions, 1977.

— MOURE, Eirin, *Sheep's Vigil by a fervent person: A translation of Alberto Caeiro / Fernando Pessoa's 'O guardador de rebanhos'*. Toronto: House of Anansi Press, 2001

— QUINTANILHA, F.E.G.: *Fernando Pessoa. Sixty Portuguese Poems*. Cardiff: University of Wales Press, 1971. Bilingual.

— RICKARD, Peter: *Fernando Pessoa. Selected Poems*. Edinburgh: Edinburgh University Press, 1971. [70 poems] Bilingual.

— ZENITH, Richard: *Selected Poems of Fernando Pessoa & Co.* New York: Harcourt Brace, 1996.

— ZENITH, Richard: *Fernando Pessoa: A Little Larger than the Entire Universe. Selected Poems*. London and New York: Penguin, 2006

Prose

— COSTA, Margaret Jull: *Fernando Pessoa. The Book of Disquiet*. London: Serpent's Tail, 1991 [259 fragments].

— HONIG, Edwin: *Always Astonished. Selected Prose by Fernando Pessoa*. San Francisco: City Lights Books, 1988 ['The Anarchist Banker' and other sundry fragments].

— LISBOA, Eugénio (with TAYLOR, L.C.) (eds.) *A Centenary Pessoa*. Manchester: Carcanet, 1995. [mostly fragments from Pessoa's theoretical writings].

— MAC ADAM, Alfred: *Fernando Pessoa. The Book of Disquiet*. New York: Pantheon Books, 1991. [276 fragments].

— RITCHIE, George: *Fernando Pessoa. 'The Mariner'. A 'static drama' in one act'*. In *Translation*, XXV, New York, Spring 1991.

— WATSON, Iain: *Fernando Pessoa. The Book of Disquiet. A Selection*. London: Quartet Books, 1991. [141 fragments].

— ZENITH, Richard: *Fernando Pessoa. The Book of Disquietude*. Manchester: Carcanet Press, 1991. [532 fragments (complete)].

— ZENITH, Richard: *Fernando Pessoa. The Book of Disquiet*. London and New York: Penguin Books, 2001 [481 fragments plus anthology of named fragments].

— ZENITH, Richard: *The Selected Prose of Fernando Pessoa*. New York: Grove Press, 2001.

— ZENITH, Richard: *The Education of the Stoic: The Only Manuscript of the Baron of Teive*. Cambridge, MA: Exact Change, 2006.

Criticism and Other Works

(A comprehensive bibliography of English criticism and a list of 50 key Portuguese texts has been compiled by José Blanco and can be found in *A Centenary Pessoa* published by Carcanet).

— BLANCO, José: *Fernando Pessoa. Esboço de uma bibliografia.* Lisbon: Imprensa Nacional/Casa de Moeda, 1983.

— COELHO, Jacinto do Prado: *Diversidade e unidade em Fernando Pessoa.* Lisbon: Ed.Verbo, 1950.

— GIL, José: *Fernando Pessoa ou la métaphysique des sensations.* Paris: Editions de la Différance, 1988.

— LOPES, Teresa Rita: *Fernando Pessoa et le drame symboliste. Hèritage et création.* Paris: Fondation Calouste Gulbenkian, 1985.

— LOPES, Teresa Rita: *Pessoa por conhecer. I—roteiro para uma expedição. II—textos para um novo mapa* (2 vols). Lisbon: Editorial Estampa, 1990.

— LOURENÇO, Eduardo: *Fernando Pessoa revisitado. Leitura estruturante do drama em gente.* Lisbon: Moraes, 1981.

— LOURENÇO, Eduardo: *Fernando, rei de nossa baviera.* Lisbon: Imprensa Nacional/Casa de Moeda, 1986.

— MONTEIRO, Adolfo Casais: *A poesia de Fernando Pessoa.* Lisbon: Imprensa Nacional/Casa da Moeda, 1985.

— MONTEIRO, George. (ed.) *The Man Who Never Was. Essays on Fernando Pessoa.* Providence, Rhode Island: Gávea-Brown, 1982.

— MONTEIRO, George: *Fernando Pessoa and Nineteenth-century Anglo-American Literature.* Lexington, KY:The University Press of Kentucky, 2000.

— PAZ, Octavio:'Unknown to Himself' in *A Centenary Pessoa.* Manchester: Carcanet, 1995.

— SARAMAGO José: *The Year of the Death of Ricardo Reis.* Translated by Giovanni Pontiero, London: Harvill, 1992.

— SENA, Jorge de: *Fernando Pessoa & Cª. heterónima.* (2 vols). Lisbon: Edições 70, 1982.

— SIMÕES, João Gaspar: *Vida e obra de Fernando Pessoa.* Lisbon: Publicações Dom Quixote, 1991.

— SOUSA, João Rui de: *Fotobibliografia de Fernando Pessoa.* Lisbon: Imprensa Nacional/Casa da Moeda, 1988.

— TABUCCHI, Antonio: *Pessoana minima.* Lisbon: Imprensa Nacional/Casa da Moeda, 1984.